UTAH
BUCKET LIST

Set Off on **120 Epic Adventures** and Discover
Incredible Destinations to Live Out Your Dreams
While Creating Unforgettable Memories
that Will Last a Lifetime.

**(Online Digital MAP included - access it through
the link provided in the MAP Chapter of this book)**

BeCrePress Travel

UTAH BUCKET LIST

UTAH BUCKET LIST

TABLE OF CONTENTS

UTAH BUCKET LIST

UTAH BUCKET LIST

UTAH BUCKET LIST

UTAH BUCKET LIST

INTRODUCTION

Welcome to *Utah Bucket List: Set Off on 120 Epic Adventures and Discover Incredible Destinations to Live Out Your Dreams*—your ultimate guide to exploring the most awe-inspiring places the Beehive State has to offer! Get ready to embark on a journey that will ignite your sense of adventure and leave you with unforgettable memories to treasure for a lifetime. This isn't just any travel guide—it's a doorway into the heart of Utah, a state where ancient landscapes, thrilling adventures, and timeless history come together to create experiences like no other.

Imagine standing beneath the towering arches of red rock in Arches National Park, or gazing over the endless expanse of the Bonneville Salt Flats, shimmering in the desert heat. Picture yourself hiking the breathtaking trails of Zion National Park, feeling the rush of wind on your face as you stand at the edge of Bryce Canyon, or losing yourself in the quiet beauty of Antelope Island as bison roam in the distance. Whether you're drawn to the wild beauty of the national parks, the fascinating history preserved in ancient petroglyphs, or the lively energy of Utah's mountain towns, this guide will take you on a journey that will leave you dreaming of your next adventure.

To make your travels effortless, each of the 120 destinations in this book is meticulously curated to give you all the details you need. Every spot you visit will include:

- **A description of the destination:** We'll bring each place to life with rich descriptions that capture the magic of Utah's landscapes, from the surreal beauty of Goblin Valley's rock formations to the serene shores of Lake Powell.

- **The address:** We've included the exact address so there's no confusion when you're planning your trip. You'll know precisely where to go, making it easy to find even the most tucked-away gems.

- **The nearest city:** To help you understand where each destination is located, you'll also find the nearest city. This gives you a sense of where you are in relation to larger hubs, helping you better organize your travels.

- **GPS coordinates:** Gone are the days of getting lost! With the exact GPS coordinates ready to plug into your favorite navigation app, you can set off on your adventure with confidence, knowing that every turn will take you where you need to go.

- **The best time to visit**: Timing is everything. Whether you want to beat the heat in the desert or catch the fall colors in the mountains, we've included the best time of year to visit each destination. That way, you can plan for the most optimal experience possible.

- **Tolls, access fees**: Some places are free, and others require a small fee. Don't worry—we'll let you know all the details about access costs, so there are no surprises when you arrive.

- **Did you know?:** To make your visit even more interesting, each destination comes with a fun fact or piece of trivia that adds a little extra layer of intrigue. Whether it's a quirky historical tidbit or a fascinating natural fact, you'll walk away with stories to share.

- **Website**: Keep yourself up to date by checking the provided websites. Whether you're looking for operating hours, special events, or updates about the destination, these links ensure you have the latest information right at your fingertips.

And that's not all! As a special bonus, this guide comes with an **interactive State Map** pre-loaded with all 120 destinations. This user-friendly map is your digital compass, helping you visualize and plan your route effortlessly. No more flipping through pages or struggling to plot out your next stop—this map has done the work for you, ensuring your Utah adventure is as smooth as the drive down Scenic Byway 12.

Utah is a land of contrasts, where the quiet of the desert is punctuated by the majestic rise of the Rocky Mountains, and the mysteries of ancient civilizations lie just beneath the surface of modern-day cities. Whether you're hiking through iconic canyons, exploring remote desert landscapes, or standing in awe before natural wonders, this state promises to captivate your imagination and leave you craving more. From thrilling outdoor adventures to peaceful moments of solitude, from cultural explorations to stargazing under Utah's pristine skies, this book will guide you through experiences that will make your heart race and your soul sing.

So, what are you waiting for? Strap on your hiking boots, charge your camera, and get ready to embark on 120 epic adventures across Utah! This is more than just a bucket list—it's a call to step out of the ordinary and dive headfirst into the extraordinary. The landscapes, the history, the wonder—it's all here, just waiting for you. Adventure is calling—are you ready to answer? Let's go!

ABOUT UTAH

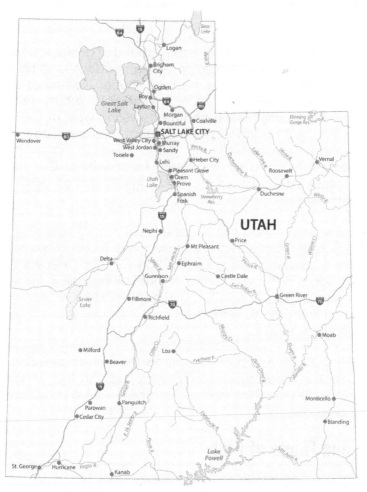

To access the Digital Map, please refer to the 'Map Chapter' in this book

Landscape of Utah

Utah's landscape is a masterpiece of nature, sculpted over millions of years by wind, water, and time. The sheer diversity of the terrain makes it one of the most awe-inspiring places in the world, a land where towering red rock formations rise against a backdrop of deep blue skies and expansive deserts give way to lush forests and snow-capped mountains. Imagine standing at the edge of a canyon, the sun casting golden hues over jagged cliffs, or wandering through vast, open valleys where silence envelops you, broken only by the distant echo of a hawk's cry.

The southern part of the state is a playground of geological wonders, where you'll find striking arches, towering hoodoos, and narrow slot canyons carved into vibrant sandstone. Places like Arches and Zion National Parks showcase nature's incredible artistry, with rock formations like Delicate Arch and the towering walls of The Narrows offering a sense of wonder and scale that must be experienced to be believed. Meanwhile, the vast, alien-like landscapes of Monument Valley and the wave-like formations at Coyote Buttes evoke a sense of timelessness, transporting visitors to a world that feels almost otherworldly.

As you move north, Utah's landscape transforms into alpine splendor, with the majestic Wasatch and Uinta Mountains providing year-round beauty and adventure. Ski resorts like Park City and Deer Valley boast powdery slopes in the winter and verdant hiking trails in the summer. The Bonneville Salt Flats offer a surreal, endless white expanse, shimmering in the heat, while the Great Salt Lake spreads out like a shimmering inland sea.

From the stunning red rock deserts to the lush forests and alpine peaks, Utah's landscape is a playground for the imagination, beckoning adventurers, dreamers, and nature lovers alike to explore its boundless beauty.

Flora and Fauna of Utah

Utah's flora and fauna are as diverse and awe-inspiring as its landscapes, with ecosystems ranging from arid deserts to alpine forests, offering a rich tapestry of life for nature lovers to explore. Picture the towering red rocks of the desert contrasted with the delicate blooms of desert wildflowers, or imagine standing in a lush alpine meadow, surrounded by aspen groves and wild sagebrush, with the snow-capped peaks of the Wasatch or Uinta Mountains in the background.

UTAH BUCKET LIST

Utah's plant life reflects the state's unique geography, with hardy species like juniper, pinyon pines, and yucca dominating the arid regions, while alpine zones are filled with towering firs, aspens, and vibrant seasonal wildflowers.

In the desert, the flora is designed for survival, with prickly pear cacti, blackbrush, and creosote bush dotting the landscape. As you move higher into the mountain regions, forests of Ponderosa pine and Douglas fir create a dramatic change in scenery, offering shaded retreats and abundant greenery. In spring and summer, the meadows burst into color, with columbine, lupine, and Indian paintbrush painting the hillsides in hues of purple, pink, and red.

Utah's fauna is equally fascinating, and as you explore the state's parks and wilderness areas, you'll encounter an impressive array of wildlife. Imagine spotting a herd of bighorn sheep navigating the rocky cliffs of Zion National Park or catching a glimpse of a mule deer grazing in a quiet meadow at sunrise. The iconic American bison roam freely on Antelope Island, while pronghorn antelope can be seen sprinting across the plains. In the higher elevations, you may even spot a black bear, mountain lion, or elusive bobcat.

Birdwatchers will delight in Utah's avian diversity, from the majestic golden eagles soaring high above the canyons to the strikingly pink hues of the American flamingos that occasionally visit the Great Salt Lake. Raptors, hawks, and peregrine falcons thrive in the state's cliffs and open spaces, while wetlands attract great blue herons, pelicans, and various waterfowl.

From the resilience of the desert's flora to the rich wildlife that roams the state's diverse ecosystems, Utah's flora and fauna offer a vibrant, ever-changing backdrop to the adventurer's journey. Each season reveals a new chapter in the story of life, with beauty waiting to be discovered in every corner.

Climate of Utah

Utah's climate is as diverse and stunning as its landscape, offering something for every adventurer, no matter the season. Imagine the crisp mountain air on a sunny winter day as you glide down powder-covered slopes in Park City, or picture the warmth of the desert sun embracing you as you hike through the mesmerizing red rock canyons of Zion or Arches National Park in the spring. Utah's climate spans the extremes, from the arid, sun-soaked deserts of the south to the snow-laden peaks in the north, creating an ever-changing palette of weather and experiences.

In the summer, Utah's desert regions, like the stunning Bryce Canyon and Monument Valley, experience hot days with temperatures soaring into the 90s (32-37°C), but the dry air keeps the heat more manageable. These areas are ideal for morning and evening explorations, where the golden light paints the landscapes in dramatic hues. High-altitude areas, such as Cedar Breaks National Monument and the Wasatch Mountains, offer a cool escape from the heat, with alpine meadows bursting into bloom under the summer sun.

Winters in Utah are a skier's paradise, with the northern regions blanketed in some of the best snow on earth. Resorts like Deer Valley and Brian Head come alive with snow lovers, while the lower elevations remain mild enough for outdoor adventures. The southern parks, like Zion, offer a quieter, cooler experience, where the vibrant reds of the cliffs contrast with the crisp, cool air.

Spring and fall are Utah's sweet spots—perfect for exploring the national parks without the intense heat or cold. These transitional seasons bring comfortable temperatures, making them ideal for scenic drives along Highway 12 or hiking iconic trails like Angel's Landing in Zion. Whether you're chasing the snow or seeking the sun, Utah's climate invites you to discover its beauty in every season, offering endless opportunities for adventure and wonder.

History of Utah

Utah's history is a vibrant story of ancient civilizations, pioneering spirit, and cultural resilience, set against a backdrop of some of the most stunning landscapes in the world. Long before Utah became a state, its lands were home to Native American cultures whose presence is still etched into the earth in the form of petroglyphs, cliff dwellings, and ancient artifacts. The Ancestral Puebloans and Fremont people, early inhabitants of the region, left behind fascinating remnants of their societies, with places like Capitol Reef and the Fremont

Petroglyphs serving as powerful reminders of their once-thriving cultures.

As you explore Utah's history, you can almost hear the whispers of these early peoples who lived in harmony with the land, building complex communities in the cliffs and valleys, surviving the harsh desert environment. In fact, the evidence of their existence can still be seen today at places like the Anasazi State Park Museum, where artifacts and ruins offer a glimpse into their lives. These early cultures would eventually give way to the modern-day Ute, Paiute, Navajo, and Goshute tribes, who have called Utah home for centuries, shaping the cultural landscape in powerful ways.

In 1776, Utah's story intersected with European explorers when Spanish priests Dominguez and Escalante set out on an expedition in search of a route between Santa Fe and California. Their journey took them through the rugged lands of Utah, and although they didn't succeed in their mission, their records laid the foundation for future explorers who would venture into this vast and unknown territory. It wasn't until the early 1800s, however, that fur trappers and mountain men began to make their mark, establishing trade routes and settlements in the region.

The defining chapter in Utah's history, though, came in 1847, when Brigham Young led the first group of Mormon pioneers into the Salt Lake Valley. After facing intense persecution in the eastern United States, the Church of Jesus Christ of Latter-day Saints sought a new homeland, and when Young arrived and famously declared, "This is the place," the course of Utah's future was forever altered. The Mormons set about creating a self-sustaining community, braving the harsh conditions of the Great Basin and transforming the desert into a thriving agricultural hub. Salt Lake City, now the state's bustling capital, grew out of this pioneering spirit, and landmarks such as Temple Square and the Salt Lake Utah Temple stand as symbols of the perseverance and faith that defined these early settlers.

The journey of the Mormon pioneers is a story of survival and hope, and today, visitors can explore this legacy at places like This is the Place Heritage Park, where the arrival of Brigham Young and his followers is commemorated. These settlers built communities throughout Utah, developing irrigation systems, constructing homes, and planting crops in what seemed to be an unforgiving landscape. Over time, their settlements expanded, and Utah became a central part of the westward expansion of the United States.

The arrival of the transcontinental railroad in 1869 at Promontory Summit, celebrated at the Golden Spike National Historical Park, marked another pivotal moment in Utah's history. The completion of the railroad not only connected the country from coast to coast but also opened Utah to a flood of new settlers, industries, and cultural influences. Mining booms followed, as rich deposits of silver, copper, and other minerals were discovered in the region, transforming small towns into bustling centers of commerce and industry. Mining towns like Park City sprang up almost overnight, and their histories can still be felt today as you walk along the charming streets of the Park City Main Street Historic District.

As Utah transitioned into the 20th century, its growth continued, with industries such as mining, agriculture, and railroads playing a key role in its economic development. But it was the state's stunning natural beauty that began to draw the attention of the nation, as adventurous travelers flocked to see its majestic red rock canyons, towering arches, and expansive deserts. In 1919, Zion National Park was established as Utah's first national park, setting the stage for the state's legacy as an outdoor adventure mecca. Today, the breathtaking landscapes of Bryce Canyon, Arches, Canyonlands, and Capitol Reef continue to captivate visitors from around the world.

Utah's natural wonders are not only a testament to its geological history but also to the Native American cultures that have revered these lands for centuries. Sites like Monument Valley Navajo Tribal Park hold deep spiritual significance, while the Fremont Petroglyphs and other rock art sites offer an intimate connection to the ancient peoples who called these lands home long before European settlers arrived.

The 20th century also saw Utah play a significant role in military history. Hill Aerospace Museum, for instance, showcases Utah's contributions to air power during World War II and beyond, while Union Station in Ogden provides a glimpse into the state's railroading past, a critical part of its industrial heritage.

UTAH BUCKET LIST

Utah's rich cultural history isn't limited to its early settlers and industrial pioneers. The state has fostered a vibrant arts scene, with institutions like the Natural History Museum of Utah and the Utah Museum of Fine Arts contributing to its cultural identity. As you wander through the state's historical sites, you'll find that Utah's history is alive in its architecture, landscapes, and communities, blending the old with the new in ways that continue to inspire.

Utah officially became the 45th state of the United States in 1896, after a long struggle for statehood that was deeply intertwined with the unique religious and cultural fabric of the region. Today, the state is a dynamic mix of old and new, where ancient history and pioneering legacies meet modern growth and innovation.

From the ancient cliff dwellings of the Ancestral Puebloans to the breathtaking national parks, from the story of the Mormon pioneers to the rise of mining towns and the building of the transcontinental railroad, Utah's history is one of exploration, resilience, and transformation. It's a history that you can feel in every canyon, every mountain, and every small town, inviting you to experience the incredible journey that shaped this remarkable state.

How to Use this Guide

Welcome to your comprehensive guide to exploring Utah! This chapter is dedicated to helping you understand how to effectively use this guide and the interactive map to enhance your travel experience. Let's dive into the simple steps to navigate the book and utilize the digital tools provided, ensuring you have the best adventure possible.

Understanding the Guide's Structure

The guide features 120 of the best destinations across the beautiful state of Utah, thoughtfully compiled to inspire and facilitate your explorations. These destinations are divided into areas and listed alphabetically. This organization aims to simplify your search process, making it quick and intuitive to locate each destination in the book.

Using the Alphabetical Listings

Since the destination areas are arranged alphabetically, you can easily flip through the guide to find a specific place or browse areas that catch your interest. Each destination entry in the book includes essential information such as:

- A vivid description of the destination.

- The complete address and the nearest major city, giving you a quick geographical context.

- GPS coordinates for precise navigation.

- The best times to visit, helping you plan your trip according to seasonal attractions and weather.

- Details on tolls or access fees, preparing you for any costs associated with your visit.

- Fun trivia to enhance your knowledge and appreciation of each location.

- A link to the official website for up-to-date information.

To further enhance your experience and save time, you can scan these website links using apps like Google Lens to open them directly without the need to type them into a browser. This seamless integration allows for quicker access to the latest information and resources about each destination.

Navigating with the Interactive State Map

Your guide comes equipped with an innovative tool—an interactive map of Utah that integrates seamlessly with Google Maps. This digital map is pre-loaded with all 120 destinations, offering an effortless way to visualize and plan your journey across the state.

How to Use the Map:

- **Open the Interactive Map**: Start by accessing the digital map through the link provided in your guide. You can open it on any device that supports Google Maps, such as a smartphone, tablet, or computer.

- **Choose Your Starting Point:** Decide where you will begin your adventure. You might start from your current location or another specific point in Utah.

- **Explore Nearby Destinations:** With the map open, zoom in and out to view the destinations near your starting point. Click on any marker to see a brief description and access quick links for navigation and more details.

- **Plan Your Itinerary:** Based on the destinations close to your chosen start, you can create a personalized itinerary. You can select multiple locations to visit in a day or plan a more extended road trip through various regions.

Combining the Book and Map for Best Results

To get the most out of your adventures:

- <u>Cross-Reference</u>: Use the interactive map to spot destinations you are interested in and then refer back to the guidebook for detailed information and insights.

- <u>Plan Sequentially:</u> As you plan your route on the map, use the alphabetical listing in the book to easily gather information on each destination and organize your visits efficiently.

- <u>Stay Updated:</u> Regularly check the provided website links for any changes in operation hours, fees, or special events at the destinations.

By following these guidelines and utilizing both the guidebook and the interactive map, you will be well-equipped to explore Utah's diverse landscapes and attractions.

Whether you are seeking solitude in nature, adventure in the outdoors, or cultural experiences in urban settings, this guide will serve as your reliable companion, ensuring every adventure is memorable and every discovery is enriching. Happy travels!

Arches National Park

Arches National Park Scenic Drive

Find your sense of adventure and exploration on the Arches National Park Scenic Drive, a must-see journey through one of Utah's natural wonders. Spanning 36 miles, this drive offers stunning views of over 2,000 natural stone arches and other geological formations. Located near Moab, this park provides a breathtaking backdrop of the high desert, with opportunities for photography, hiking, and simply enjoying the beauty of nature's handiwork. From the iconic Delicate Arch to the towering Courthouse Towers, every turn on this drive unveils awe-inspiring scenery. Don't forget to bring your camera to capture these unforgettable sights!

Location: PC2P+G5 Moab, Utah

Closest City or Town: Moab, Utah

How to Get There: From Moab, drive north on US-191 for about 5 miles. Turn right onto Arches Entrance Road and follow it into the park.

GPS Coordinates: 38.7013125° N, 109.5645625° W

Best Time to Visit: Spring and fall for mild weather and fewer crowds

Pass/Permit/Fees: $30 per vehicle for a 7-day pass

Did You Know? Arches National Park contains the world's largest concentration of natural sandstone arches.

Website: https://www.discovermoab.com/

Delicate Arch

Discover the stunning elegance of Delicate Arch, perhaps Utah's most famous natural landmark. This 52-foot-tall free-standing arch is located in the eastern part of Arches National Park and has become a symbol of the state itself. The hike to Delicate Arch is a 3-mile round trip that rewards you with an unforgettable view of this natural marvel. As you journey across rolling terrain and slick rock, the anticipation builds until the arch appears, framed against the La Sal

Mountains. Sunset is a particularly magical time to visit, as the arch glows brilliantly under the desert sky.

Location: PFPH+5P Castle Valley, Utah

Closest City or Town: Moab, Utah

How to Get There: From the Arches National Park entrance, drive 11.5 miles on the main park road, then turn right onto Wolfe Ranch Road. The trailhead begins at Wolfe Ranch.

GPS Coordinates: 38.7354375° N, 109.5206875° W

Best Time to Visit: Spring and fall for the best hiking conditions

Pass/Permit/Fees: Included in Arches National Park entrance fee

Did You Know? Delicate Arch is featured on Utah's state license plate.

Website: https://www.nps.gov/arch/planyourvisit/delicate-arch.htm

Double Arch

Step into the surreal world of Double Arch, where two gigantic natural arches share a common foundation. This geological wonder can be found in the Windows Section of Arches National Park, making it a short and easy stroll from the parking area. As you approach these twin arches, their sheer size and proximity to one another are certain to leave you in awe. This area is perfect for exploring, climbing, and taking photographs, with the impressive formations providing a natural frame for the blue sky above. The Double Arch is also notable for having the tallest opening in the park.

Location: The Windows Rd, Arches National Park, UT 84532

Closest City or Town: Moab, Utah

How to Get There: From Moab, head north on US-191 for 5 miles, then turn right into Arches National Park. Follow the main park road for 9 miles and turn right onto Windows Road.

GPS Coordinates: 38.6916170° N, 109.5403916° W

Best Time to Visit: Early morning or late afternoon for optimal lighting

Pass/Permit/Fees: Included in Arches National Park entrance fee

Did You Know? Double Arch features prominently in the opening scenes of Indiana Jones and the Last Crusade.

Website: https://www.nps.gov/arch/index.htm

Fiery Furnace

Find your sense of adventure in the labyrinthine passageways of Fiery Furnace, an intricate maze of narrow canyons and towering rock fins. This unique section of Arches National Park in Moab requires a bit more preparation and skill to navigate, but the reward is an unforgettable exploration of a landscape that feels almost otherworldly. Guided tours led by park rangers offer fascinating insights into the area's geology and ecology, while self-guided permits are available for those seeking a more independent challenge. The glowing red rocks of the Fiery Furnace come alive under the setting sun, creating a visual spectacle you won't forget.

Location: PCVM+8G Moab, Utah

Closest City or Town: Moab, Utah

How to Get There: From the Arches National Park entrance, drive 14.4 miles on the main park road. The Fiery Furnace parking area will be on your right.

GPS Coordinates: 38.7433125° N, 109.5661875° W

Best Time to Visit: Spring and fall for cooler temperatures and less intense sunlight

Pass/Permit/Fees: $6 per person for guided tours; self-guided permits require a $10 fee

Did You Know? The Fiery Furnace is named for the reddish glow the rocks emanate during sunset.

Website: https://www.nps.gov/arch/planyourvisit/fiery-furnace.htm

BIG WATER

Lone Rock Beach

Enjoy a unique beachside experience at Lone Rock Beach, a pristine spot located on the shores of Lake Powell. This expansive sandy beach offers stunning views of the monumental Lone Rock, a towering sandstone butte that rises dramatically from the water. Situated in the Glen Canyon National Recreation Area, this beach is perfect for swimming, kayaking, and camping right by the water's edge. Whether you're looking to bask in the sun or explore the surrounding waters by boat, Lone Rock Beach promises an exciting yet relaxing day out in nature, with picturesque sunsets reflecting off the lake's serene surface.

Location: Lone Rock Road, Big Water, UT 84741

Closest City or Town: Big Water, Utah

How to Get There: From Page, Arizona, drive north on US-89 for about 12 miles. Turn left onto Lone Rock Road and follow it to the beach access.

GPS Coordinates: 37.0168804° N, 111.5414331° W

Best Time to Visit: Late spring to early fall for swimming and boating

Pass/Permit/Fees: $30 per vehicle for a 7-day pass, free for annual pass holders

Did You Know? Lone Rock Beach offers one of the few places where you can camp directly on the sandy beach in the area.

Website: https://www.nps.gov/glca/planyourvisit/camping.htm

The Wave at Coyote Buttes

Embark on an awe-inspiring adventure to The Wave at Coyote Buttes, an unparalleled sandstone rock formation in the Paria Canyon-Vermilion Cliffs Wilderness. Marvel at the undulating patterns that create a surreal, photogenic landscape. Situated on the Arizona-Utah border, The Wave's striking red rock swirls are a photographer's dream and a hiker's paradise. Traverse the challenging trail to experience a natural wonder that feels out of this world.

Location: The Wave Trail, Kanab, AZ 84741

Closest City or Town: Kanab, Arizona

How to Get There: From Kanab, head east on US-89 for about 34 miles. Then turn south onto House Rock Valley Road and follow for 8.4 miles to the Wire Pass Trailhead.

GPS Coordinates: 37.0088263° N, 112.0067376° W

Best Time to Visit: Spring and Fall for the most pleasant hiking conditions

Pass/Permit/Fees: A permit is required through a lottery system (@ $9.00 per person/day)

Did You Know? The formation of The Wave began during the Jurassic period, around 190 million years ago.

Website: https://www.thewave.info/

BLANDING

Goosenecks State Park

Discover dramatic vistas at Goosenecks State Park, where the San Juan River carves deep, twisting meanders into the landscape. This geological spectacle, resembling a series of tight loops, offers sweeping views of one of the most impressive examples of entrenched river meanders in the world. Nestled in southeastern Utah, this park provides a condensed panorama of nature's artistry. Explore the stunning overlook and witness millions of years of geological history etched into the earth.

Location: Sr 316, Blanding, UT 84531

Closest City or Town: Blanding, Utah

How to Get There: Travel southwest on US-191 S from Blanding. Turn west onto UT-95, then south on UT-261, and follow signs for Goosenecks State Park.

GPS Coordinates: 37.6241646° N, 109.4781770° W

Best Time to Visit: Year-round, but spring and fall offer milder temperatures

Pass/Permit/Fees: $5 per vehicle day-use fee

Did You Know? The river has cut down over 1,000 feet to create the goosenecks, yet travels only about one mile as the crow flies.

Website: http://stateparks.utah.gov/parks/goosenecks

BLUFF

Bluff Fort Historic Site

Step back in time at Bluff Fort Historic Site, a living history museum celebrating the pioneer spirit. Located in the rustic town of Bluff, this site features restored cabins, artifacts, and engaging exhibits that tell the story of the Mormon pioneers who settled the area in 1880. Wander through the historical buildings, ride in a covered wagon, and immerse yourself in the authentic pioneer experience.

Location: 550 E Black Locust Ave, Bluff, UT 84512-7720

Closest City or Town: Bluff, Utah

How to Get There: From US-191, turn east onto Black Locust Ave and continue until you reach Bluff Fort.

GPS Coordinates: 37.2841898° N, 109.5526624° W

Best Time to Visit: Spring and Fall for the best weather conditions

Pass/Permit/Fees: Free admission, donations welcomed

Did You Know? The site commemorates the "Hole-in-the-Rock" expedition, a challenging journey the settlers undertook to reach Bluff in 1880.

Website: https://bluffutah.org/bluff-fort/

BOULDER

Anasazi State Park Museum

Uncover ancient history at Anasazi State Park Museum, home to one of the largest Ancestral Puebloan village sites in Utah. Nestled in the scenic town of Boulder, this museum offers insights into the lives and culture of the Anasazi people who inhabited the region over a thousand years ago. Explore the museum's artifacts, visit the partially excavated Coomb's Site, and take a stroll along the interpretive trails.

Location: 460 Ut-12, Boulder, UT 84716

Closest City or Town: Boulder, Utah

How to Get There: Follow UT-12 E from Escalante to Boulder, the museum is located right on the highway.

GPS Coordinates: 37.9108361° N, 111.4236296° W

Best Time to Visit: Open year-round; spring and fall offer the most pleasant weather

Pass/Permit/Fees: $5 per person

Did You Know? The Coomb's Site, part of the museum, was home to as many as 200 people and dates back over 800 years.

Website: https://www.facebook.com/AnasaziStatePark/

BRIAN HEAD

Brian Head Resort

Find year-round adventure at Brian Head Resort, Utah's premier alpine destination. Nestled in the stunning Dixie National Forest, this resort offers world-class skiing and snowboarding in the winter, and miles of mountain biking and hiking trails in the summer. Known for its exceptional snowfall, Brian Head boasts the highest base elevation in Utah at 9,600 feet. It's the ultimate playground for outdoor enthusiasts.

Location: 329 South Highway 143, Brian Head, UT 84719

Closest City or Town: Brian Head, Utah

How to Get There: From Interstate 15, take the Parowan exit, follow UT-143 S directly to Brian Head.

GPS Coordinates: 37.7021135° N, 112.8499780° W

Best Time to Visit: Winter for snow activities; Summer for biking and hiking

Pass/Permit/Fees: Varies by activity. Please visit the resort's website for details.

Did You Know? The resort is named after a nearby peak called Brian Head Peak, which stands at 11,307 feet.

Website: https://www.brianhead.com/

BRYCE

Bryce Wildlife Adventure

Find your sense of wonder at Bryce Wildlife Adventure, where nature and excitement blend in perfect harmony in Bryce, Utah. Nestled in the sagebrush-covered landscape of Highway 12, this destination offers an eclectic wildlife museum and thrilling outdoor experiences. Encounter mounted wildlife exhibits and guided ATV rides through the surrounding scenery ensure an immersive adventure.

Location: 1945 Utah 12, Bryce, UT 84764

Closest City or Town: Bryce, Utah

How to Get There: From Bryce Canyon City, head east on Utah State Route 12 for about 1.5 miles. Bryce Wildlife Adventure is on your right.

GPS Coordinates: 37.7007149° N, 112.1975817° W

Best Time to Visit: Spring through fall for optimal weather and wildlife activity.

Pass/Permit/Fees: Admission to the museum varies; outdoor activities may have separate fees. Check the website for details.

Did You Know? The museum boasts over 800 mounted animals from around the world, offering an in-depth look at diverse wildlife.

Website: https://www.brycewildlifeadventure.com/museum-tickets/

BRYCE CANYON NATIONAL PARK

Bryce Canyon National Park

Dive into the awe-inspiring Bryce Canyon National Park, a geological wonderland in southwestern Utah. Its iconic spire-shaped rock formations, known as hoodoos, create a landscape that's nothing short of magical. Explore a variety of hiking trails that lead you through this stunning amphitheater of rock formations, where every twist and turn reveals a new natural spectacle.

Location: JRRJ+55 Bryce Canyon City, Utah

Closest City or Town: Bryce Canyon City, Utah

How to Get There: Drive north on UT-63 from Bryce Canyon City for approximately 3 miles to reach the park entrance.

GPS Coordinates: 37.6404299° N, 112.1695870° W

Best Time to Visit: May to September for warm temperatures and clear skies.

Pass/Permit/Fees: $35 per vehicle for a 7-day pass. Check the website for more options.

Did You Know? Bryce Canyon has the largest concentration of hoodoos on Earth, creating a truly unique geological site.

Website: http://www.nps.gov/brca/index.htm

Bryce Canyon Scenic Drive

Discover the breathtaking vistas of Bryce Canyon Scenic Drive, a must-see route through one of Utah's most iconic landscapes. Stretching nearly 38 miles round-trip, this drive offers numerous overlooks with stunning views of the rugged terrain. Don't miss key points like Sunrise Point, Sunset Point, and Rainbow Point for unparalleled photo opportunities and moments of serene beauty.

Location: W 300 S, Bryce Canyon City, UT 84764

Closest City or Town: Bryce Canyon City, Utah

How to Get There: Begin the drive by heading south on UT-63 from Bryce Canyon City. The scenic route starts just past the park entrance.

GPS Coordinates: 37.7001604° N, 112.1952391° W

Best Time to Visit: Late spring to early fall for favorable weather conditions and clear visibility.

Pass/Permit/Fees: Included with park entrance fee ($35 per vehicle for a 7-day pass).

Did You Know? The scenic drive reaches elevations of up to 9,100 feet, providing some of the highest vantage points in the park.

Website: https://www.americansouthwest.net/utah/mexican_hat/muley_point.html

Bryce Point

Soak in the panoramic views from Bryce Point, one of the most celebrated overlooks in Bryce Canyon National Park. Situated on the park's southern edge, this vantage point provides sweeping views of the Bryce Amphitheater and its mesmerizing hoodoos that seem to glow with the changing light of dawn and dusk.

Location: JR3V+Q9 Tropic, Utah

Closest City or Town: Tropic, Utah

How to Get There: From the park entrance, drive south on UT-63, then turn left onto Rim Road and follow signage to Bryce Point.

GPS Coordinates: 37.6043935° N, 112.1565495° W

Best Time to Visit: Early morning for sunrise views or late afternoon for evening light.

Pass/Permit/Fees: Included in the Bryce Canyon National Park entrance fee ($35 per vehicle for a 7-day pass).

Did You Know? Bryce Point offers some of the best views for photographers, especially during sunrise when the hoodoos are bathed in a warm, golden light.

Website: https://www.nps.gov/brca/planyourvisit/brycepoint.htm

Inspiration Point

Feel inspired by the dramatic vistas at Inspiration Point, one of Bryce Canyon National Park's quintessential overlooks. Set atop sheer cliffs, this viewpoint offers an uninterrupted panorama of the geological wonders below, showcasing the park's intricate maze of hoodoos and deep, colorful canyons.

Location: JR7H+VJ Bryce Canyon City, Utah

Closest City or Town: Bryce Canyon City, Utah

How to Get There: Head south on UT-63 from Bryce Canyon City, then turn onto Rim Road and follow signs to reach Inspiration Point.

GPS Coordinates: 37.6157224° N, 112.1704921° W

Best Time to Visit: Sunrise and sunset provide the most dramatic lighting for photography and viewing.

Pass/Permit/Fees: Covered by the Bryce Canyon National Park entrance fee ($35 per vehicle for a 7-day pass).

Did You Know? The view from Inspiration Point highlights the park's Silent City, a dense collection of hoodoos that resemble a city skyline.

Website: https://www.nps.gov/brca/planyourvisit/inspiration.htm

Navajo Trail

Discover the mesmerizing beauty of Bryce Canyon on the Navajo Trail, a quintessential hike showcasing the park's unique hoodoos and dramatic landscapes. As you descend through Wall Street, you'll be surrounded by towering rock formations and ancient Douglas fir trees. Located in the heart of Bryce Canyon National Park, this trail offers a remarkable opportunity to engage with nature's artistry up close. Whether you're an avid hiker or a casual explorer, the Navajo Trail promises an unforgettable adventure through one of Utah's geological marvels.

Location: JRFM+2P Bryce Canyon City, Utah

Closest City or Town: Bryce Canyon City, Utah

How to Get There: From Bryce Canyon City, head south on UT-63, enter the park, and follow signs to the Navajo Loop Trailhead.

GPS Coordinates: 37.6206402° N, 112.1637707° W

Best Time to Visit: Spring and fall for pleasant weather and fewer crowds

Pass/Permit/Fees: Included in Bryce Canyon National Park entrance fee ($35 per vehicle for a 7-day pass)

Did You Know? The Navajo Trail is named after the Navajo sandstone that forms the canyon's famous hoodoos.

Website: http://www.nps.gov/brca/planyourvisit/navajotrail.htm

Navajo/Queens Garden Loop

Combine the best of Bryce Canyon's landscapes on the Navajo/Queens Garden Loop, a trail that weaves together the highlights of the park's scenery. Start your journey on the Navajo Trail, then transition to the Queens Garden Trail where the iconic Queen Victoria hoodoo awaits. This loop delivers a captivating mix of narrow canyons, towering hoodoos, and panoramic vistas. Immerse yourself in the surreal rock formations and the serene desert atmosphere as you hike through this extraordinary natural wonder.

Location: JRCM+XH Bryce Canyon City, Utah

Closest City or Town: Bryce Canyon City, Utah

How to Get There: From Bryce Canyon City, drive south on UT-63, enter the park, and follow signs to the trailheads.

GPS Coordinates: 37.6238046° N, 112.1606402° W

Best Time to Visit: Spring and fall for the best hiking conditions

Pass/Permit/Fees: Included in Bryce Canyon National Park entrance fee ($35 per vehicle for a 7-day pass)

Did You Know? The loop is considered one of the most accessible and rewarding hikes in Bryce Canyon, accommodating a range of hiking abilities.

Website: http://www.nps.gov/brca/planyourvisit/navajotrail.htm

Queen's Garden Trail

Find your sense of wonder on the Queen's Garden Trail, a pathway that leads to some of the most enchanting formations in Bryce Canyon National Park. The trail descends into the canyon, guiding you through a landscape dotted with whimsical rock shapes, including the likeness of Queen Victoria. Ideal for a serene yet adventurous hike, the Queen's Garden Trail allows you to experience the unique beauty and tranquility of this geological wonderland.

Location: JRHP+8W Bryce Canyon City, Utah

Closest City or Town: Bryce Canyon City, Utah

How to Get There: From Bryce Canyon City, drive south on UT-63 into the park, and follow signs to the Queen's Garden Trailhead at Sunrise Point.

GPS Coordinates: 37.6238046° N, 112.1606402° W

Best Time to Visit: Spring and fall for mild temperatures

Pass/Permit/Fees: Included in Bryce Canyon National Park entrance fee ($35 per vehicle for a 7-day pass)

Did You Know? The trail is named for the hoodoo that bears a striking resemblance to Queen Victoria.

Website:
https://www.nps.gov/brca/planyourvisit/queensgarden.htm

Rainbow Point

Find your sense of awe at Rainbow Point, the highest viewpoint in Bryce Canyon National Park. Offering panoramic views of the park, including the Bryce Amphitheater and surrounding forest, this overlook is perfect for those seeking breathtaking vistas and a tranquil escape. Located at the end of the park's scenic drive, Rainbow Point also marks the trailheads for several remarkable hikes, providing a gateway to deeper exploration.

Location: 110 E Center St, Bryce Canyon City, UT 84764

Closest City or Town: Bryce Canyon City, Utah

How to Get There: Drive south on UT-63 from Bryce Canyon City, continue through the park for about 15 miles until reaching Rainbow Point.

GPS Coordinates: 37.6729858° N, 112.1540013° W

Best Time to Visit: Late spring to early fall for clear views and pleasant weather

Pass/Permit/Fees: Included in Bryce Canyon National Park entrance fee ($35 per vehicle for a 7-day pass)

Did You Know? At 9,115 feet, Rainbow Point offers a commanding view that stretches all the way to the Grand Staircase-Escalante National Monument.

Website: https://www.nps.gov/brca/planyourvisit/rainbowyovimpa.htm

Sunrise Point

Experience the magic of a new day at Sunrise Point in Bryce Canyon National Park. Overlooking the Bryce Amphitheater, this spot is renowned for its breathtaking sunrise views that cast a golden glow over the hoodoos and rock formations. Located near the park's main entrance, Sunrise Point is easily accessible and serves as a starting point for several popular trails, making it a perfect destination for both photographers and hikers.

Location: JRGJ+RQ Bryce Canyon City, Utah

Closest City or Town: Bryce Canyon City, Utah

How to Get There: From Bryce Canyon City, head south on UT-63 into the park, and follow signs to Sunrise Point.

GPS Coordinates: 37.6270625° N, 112.1680625° W

Best Time to Visit: Early morning for sunrise

Pass/Permit/Fees: Included in Bryce Canyon National Park entrance fee ($35 per vehicle for a 7-day pass)

Did You Know? From Sunrise Point, you can see famous formations such as the Boat Mesa and Sinking Ship.

Website: https://www.nps.gov/brca/planyourvisit/sunrise.htm

Sunset Point

Immerse yourself in the captivating vistas from Sunset Point, located in Bryce Canyon National Park. This viewpoint offers some of the most spectacular scenery, with panoramic views of Bryce Amphitheater's unique hoodoos glowing brilliantly under the changing light. Ideal for photography and simply soaking in the beauty, Sunset Point is a must-visit for those exploring Bryce Canyon.

Location: JRFJ+FR Tropic, Utah

Closest City or Town: Tropic, Utah

How to Get There: Drive south on UT-63 from Bryce Canyon City, then follow signs to Sunset Point.

GPS Coordinates: 37.6236875° N, 112.1679375° W

Best Time to Visit: Early morning or late afternoon for optimal lighting

Pass/Permit/Fees: Included in the Bryce Canyon National Park entrance fee ($35 per vehicle for a 7-day pass).

Did You Know? Sunset Point is especially famous for its view of the Silent City — a cluster of hoodoos resembling ancient city towers.

Website: https://www.nps.gov/brca/planyourvisit/sunset.htm

CANYONLANDS NATIONAL PARK

Grand View Point Overlook

Find your sense of wonder at Grand View Point Overlook in Canyonlands National Park. Located in the park's Island in the Sky district, this overlook offers breathtaking views of the Canyonlands' rugged terrain and expansive canyons. Hike the short, easy trail to the overlook and be rewarded with panoramic vistas that stretch for miles, making it a perfect spot for photography and quiet reflection.

Location: 843J+CV Moab, Utah

Closest City or Town: Moab, Utah

How to Get There: From Moab, drive north on US-191, then turn west onto UT-313 and follow the signs to Island in the Sky district.

GPS Coordinates: 38.3035568° N, 109.8677751° W

Best Time to Visit: Spring and fall for mild weather and clear skies

Pass/Permit/Fees: $30 per vehicle entrance fee

Did You Know? On a clear day, you can see over 100 miles to the horizon from Grand View Point.

Website: http://www.nps.gov/cany/index.htm

Island in the Sky

Discover a panoramic masterpiece at Island in the Sky, a mesa in Canyonlands National Park rising over 1,000 feet above the surrounding terrain. This lofty perch provides some of the most striking views in the park, with overlooks offering vistas of the Green and Colorado Rivers. Take a scenic drive or hike the mesa's trails for awe-inspiring views and unforgettable moments.

Location: F55H+WJ Moab, Utah

Closest City or Town: Moab, Utah

How to Get There: From Moab, drive north on US-191, turn west onto UT-313, and follow the signs to Island in the Sky.

GPS Coordinates: 38.4598125° N, 109.8209375° W

Best Time to Visit: Spring and fall for pleasant temperatures

Pass/Permit/Fees: $30 per vehicle entrance fee

Did You Know? The Island in the Sky offers some of the best stargazing opportunities due to its high elevation and remote location.

Website: http://www.nps.gov/cany/planyourvisit/islandinthesky.htm

Mesa Arch

Experience one of Utah's most iconic landmarks at Mesa Arch in Canyonlands National Park. This natural rock arch sits right at the edge of a cliff, providing a dramatic window to the vast landscape below. A short and easy hike leads you to the arch, where the rising sun creates a breathtaking glow against the sandstone— a must-see for photographers.

Location: 94QJ+MR Moab, Utah

Closest City or Town: Moab, Utah

How to Get There: From Moab, drive north on US-191, turn west onto UT-313, and follow signs to the Mesa Arch trailhead.

GPS Coordinates: 38.5733155° N, 109.5498395° W

Best Time to Visit: Early morning for the stunning sunrise light

Pass/Permit/Fees: $30 per vehicle entrance fee

Did You Know? Mesa Arch offers a perfect natural frame for photos with the distant La Sal Mountains visible through its span.

Website: https://www.nps.gov/thingstodo/cany-mesa-arch.htm

Shafer Trail

Find your off-road adventure on Shafer Trail, a thrilling 4x4 route in Canyonlands National Park. This historic trail winds down steep switchbacks and provides jaw-dropping views of the Colorado River and surrounding canyons. Ideal for those with a sense of adventure, the trail offers a challenging drive through rugged landscapes and is a favorite among experienced off-roaders.

Location: G84Q+PW, Moab, UT 84532

Closest City or Town: Moab, Utah

How to Get There: From Moab, drive north on US-191, then turn west onto UT-279 and follow signs to the Shafer Trail.

GPS Coordinates: 38.5037537° N, 109.6587373° W

Best Time to Visit: Spring and fall for mild weather

Pass/Permit/Fees: Included in the Canyonlands National Park entrance fee ($30 per vehicle)

Did You Know? Shafer Trail was originally a cattle trail used by ranchers in the early 1900s.

Website: http://www.nps.gov/cany/index.htm

CAPITOL REEF NATIONAL PARK

Capitol Reef National Park

Uncover the geological wonders of Capitol Reef National Park, a hidden gem located in south-central Utah. Often overshadowed by its more famous neighbors, this park features a stunningly diverse landscape of towering cliffs, winding canyons, and ancient monoliths. Visitors can enjoy a wide range of activities, from scenic drives and hiking to exploring historic sites. Unique to the park is the Waterpocket Fold, a 100-mile-long wrinkle in the Earth's crust that offers an awe-inspiring backdrop to any adventure.

Location: 7PRQ+H5 Torrey, Utah

Closest City or Town: Torrey, Utah

How to Get There: From Torrey, head east on UT-24 for about 11 miles to reach the park entrance.

GPS Coordinates: 38.2998050° N, 111.4189690° W

Best Time to Visit: Spring and fall for pleasant weather and fewer crowds

Pass/Permit/Fees: $20 per vehicle for a 7-day pass

Did You Know? Capitol Reef gets its name from the white Navajo Sandstone domes that resemble the U.S. Capitol building.

Website: http://www.nps.gov/care/index.htm

Fremont Petroglyphs

Journey through time as you explore the Fremont Petroglyphs, a captivating site located within Capitol Reef National Park. These ancient carvings, created by the Fremont people over a thousand years ago, tell fascinating stories through their rock art. Perfect for history enthusiasts and families, the petroglyphs are easily accessible via a short and scenic walk from the main road, offering a glimpse into the prehistoric culture that once thrived in this rugged landscape.

UTAH BUCKET LIST

Location: 52 West Headquarters Dr Fruita, Capitol Reef National Park, UT 84775

Closest City or Town: Fruita, Utah

How to Get There: Follow UT-24 east from Torrey to the Capitol Reef Visitor Center, then continue to the designated petroglyph viewing areas.

GPS Coordinates: 38.2855355° N, 111.2468360° W

Best Time to Visit: Spring and fall for mild weather conditions

Pass/Permit/Fees: Included in Capitol Reef National Park entrance fee

Did You Know? The petroglyphs feature human, animal, and abstract shapes, providing insight into the Fremont people's way of life.

Website: https://nps.gov/care/learn/historyculture/fremont.htm

CEDAR CITY

Cedar Breaks National Monument

Find your sense of adventure at Cedar Breaks National Monument, a breathtaking natural amphitheater located in southwestern Utah. This park is known for its vibrant rock formations and lush meadows, offering visitors a chance to hike among wildflowers and ancient bristlecone pines. The park's high elevation provides stunning views and cooler temperatures, making it an ideal escape in the summer months.

Location: State Highway 148, Cedar City, UT 84719

Closest City or Town: Cedar City, Utah

How to Get There: From Cedar City, drive east on UT-14 for about 18 miles, then turn left onto UT-148 to reach the park entrance.

GPS Coordinates: 37.6774769° N, 113.0618931° W

Best Time to Visit: Summer and early fall for optimal conditions

Pass/Permit/Fees: $10 per person for a 7-day pass

Did You Know? Cedar Breaks is home to some of the oldest trees on Earth, with some bristlecone pines exceeding 1,600 years.

Website: https://www.nps.gov/cebr/index.htm

Dixie National Forest

Discover the vast beauty of Dixie National Forest, stretching across south-central Utah. This expansive forest offers diverse landscapes, from the red rock formations of Red Canyon to the alpine scenery of Boulder Mountain. Outdoor enthusiasts can partake in activities like hiking, fishing, and camping, all while enjoying the serene wilderness. The forest spans several ecosystems, ensuring a unique experience with each visit.

Location: 820 N Main St, Cedar City, UT 84721

Closest City or Town: Cedar City, Utah

How to Get There: From Cedar City, take UT-14 east to access various entry points of the forest.

GPS Coordinates: 37.6914943° N, 113.0606511° W

Best Time to Visit: Spring to fall for the best outdoor activities

Pass/Permit/Fees: Most activities are free; some camping areas may require a fee

Did You Know? Dixie National Forest covers almost two million acres, making it the largest national forest in Utah.

Website: https://www.fs.usda.gov/dixie

CORINNE

Golden Spike National Historical Park

Step back in time at Golden Spike National Historical Park, where the Transcontinental Railroad was completed in 1869. Located in Promontory, Utah, this park commemorates the historic moment with reenactments, exhibits, and displays of the iconic Jupiter and No. 119 locomotives. Visitors can learn about the monumental effort that connected the east and west coasts of the United States, revolutionizing travel and commerce.

Location: 6200 N 22300 W, Corinne, UT 84307

Closest City or Town: Corinne, Utah

How to Get There: From I-15, take exit 365 and follow signs to UT-83 west, then north to the park entrance.

GPS Coordinates: 41.6171911° N, 112.5507226° W

Best Time to Visit: Late spring to early fall for outdoor activities

Pass/Permit/Fees: $10 per vehicle for a 7-day pass

Did You Know? The Golden Spike ceremony marked the completion of 1,912 miles of track that linked the Central Pacific and Union Pacific railroads.

Website: https://www.nps.gov/gosp/index.htm

DEWEY

Scenic Byway of Highway 128

Find your sense of awe on the Scenic Byway of Highway 128, a road that meanders through some of Utah's most spectacular landscapes. Located near Dewey, this route is known for its breathtaking views of the Colorado River, red rock canyons, and towering sandstone formations. Drive or cycle along this scenic highway for an unforgettable journey through rugged beauty and dramatic vistas. Don't forget to stop at the numerous pullouts to enjoy the panoramic views and snap some photos of the stunning scenery under the clear blue sky.

Location: RM6V+88, Dewey, UT 84532

Closest City or Town: Moab, Utah

How to Get There: From Moab, head northeast on US-191 and turn right onto UT-128 E. Continue for about 45 miles to experience the most scenic parts of the highway.

GPS Coordinates: 38.7012560° N, 109.3937872° W

Best Time to Visit: Spring and fall for mild weather and fewer crowds

Pass/Permit/Fees: None

Did You Know? This byway is also known as the River Road, offering views that rival those of the Grand Canyon.

Website: https://www.discovermoab.com/scenic-byway-u-128/

DRAPER

Loveland Living Planet Aquarium

Venture into the underwater world at the Loveland Living Planet Aquarium in Draper, Utah. This captivating aquarium offers a deep dive into marine life from around the globe, featuring exhibits ranging from the South American rainforest to the Antarctic Ocean. Engage with interactive displays, marvel at the giant sharks and stingrays, and explore the mesmerizing jellyfish gallery. Perfect for families and marine enthusiasts, the aquarium provides an educational yet thrilling journey under the sea.

Location: 12033 S Lone Peak Pkwy, Draper, UT 84020-9414

Closest City or Town: Draper, Utah

How to Get There: From I-15, take exit 291 for UT-71/12300 S, then turn east onto 12300 S. Turn right onto Lone Peak Parkway and follow signs to the aquarium.

GPS Coordinates: 40.5320877° N, 111.8938258° W

Best Time to Visit: Open year-round; weekdays often have fewer crowds

Pass/Permit/Fees: Admission fees apply; check website for current rates

Did You Know? The aquarium features the Deep Sea Lab, where you can explore virtual ocean depths in a remarkable digital experience.

Website: http://livingplanetaquarium.org/

ESCALANTE

Grand Staircase Escalante National Monument

Embark on a journey of discovery at Grand Staircase Escalante National Monument, a vast and geologically diverse area in southern Utah. This monument is renowned for its rugged cliffs, ancient fossils, and slot canyons waiting to be explored. Take a hike through the dramatic landscapes, go rock climbing, or embark on a guided tour to learn about the area's rich history and archaeology. It's a haven for adventurers and nature lovers alike.

Location: 151 N Main St, Glendale, UT 84729

Closest City or Town: Glendale, Utah

How to Get There: From Glendale, head north on US-89, then turn east onto UT-12 E towards Escalante. The monument's various access points are spread along this route.

GPS Coordinates: 37.3203085° N, 112.5978966° W

Best Time to Visit: Spring and fall for mild temperatures and optimal hiking conditions

Pass/Permit/Fees: None

Did You Know? The monument covers nearly 1.9 million acres, providing endless exploration opportunities.

Website: https://www.blm.gov/programs/national-conservation-lands/utah/grand-staircase-escalante-national-monument

Scenic Byway Route 12

Uncover the hidden treasures along Scenic Byway Route 12, an All-American Road that stretches through Utah's most pristine landscapes. This 123-mile route winds through alpine forests, red rock canyons, and the stunning Grand Staircase-Escalante National Monument. Whether you're driving, cycling, or simply stopping at the overlooks, this byway promises a journey rich in natural beauty and history.

UTAH BUCKET LIST

Location: Route 12, Escalante, UT 84726

Closest City or Town: Escalante, Utah

How to Get There: From Escalante, head east on UT-12 E to explore the scenic byway. The route also connects to several other parks and monuments along the way.

GPS Coordinates: 37.7702663° N, 111.6021190° W

Best Time to Visit: Late spring to early fall for the best weather

Pass/Permit/Fees: None

Did You Know? Scenic Byway Route 12 is one of the top-rated scenic byways in the United States.

Website: https://www.visitutah.com/articles/the-all-american-road-scenic-byway-12

FARMINGTON

Lagoon Amusement Park

Experience thrills and nostalgia at Lagoon Amusement Park, Utah's premier amusement destination in Farmington. This family-friendly park features a mix of classic rides, roller coasters, water attractions, and even a vintage carousel. With over 50 rides and attractions, including the daring Cannibal roller coaster and the relaxing Lagoon-A-Beach water park, Lagoon offers fun for all ages.

Location: 375 North Lagoon Dr, Farmington, UT 84025-2554

Closest City or Town: Farmington, Utah

How to Get There: From I-15, take exit 322 for Park Lane, then turn south onto Lagoon Drive and follow signs to the park.

GPS Coordinates: 40.9856936° N, 111.8948588° W

Best Time to Visit: Summer months for the full amusement park experience

Pass/Permit/Fees: Admission fees vary by season and age; check website for details

Did You Know? Lagoon Amusement Park is home to one of the oldest running roller coasters in the world, The Roller Coaster, built in 1921.

Website: http://www.lagoonpark.com/

GREEN RIVER

Goblin Valley State Park

Find your sense of adventure in Goblin Valley State Park, renowned for its alien-like landscape filled with mushroom-shaped rock formations known as hoodoos. Located near Green River, Utah, this park feels like walking on another planet, offering an otherworldly canvas perfect for hiking, photography, and exploration. You can wander the expansive valley, discovering countless goblins, each uniquely shaped by millennia of wind and water erosion. Bring your camera and your curiosity—you're in for an unforgettable journey.

Location: 18630 Goblin Valley Rd, Green River, UT 84525

Closest City or Town: Green River, Utah

How to Get There: From Green River, travel south on UT-24 for about 45 miles, then turn west onto Goblin Valley Road and follow it to the park entrance.

GPS Coordinates: 38.5779757° N, 110.7074544° W

Best Time to Visit: Spring and fall for milder weather and vibrant colors

Pass/Permit/Fees: $20 per vehicle for a day pass

Did You Know? Goblin Valley's unique landscape was featured in the 1999 sci-fi comedy film Galaxy Quest.

Website: http://stateparks.utah.gov/parks/goblin-valley/

IRVIS

Snow Canyon State Park

Immerse yourself in the serene beauty of Snow Canyon State Park, a hidden gem nestled in the red rock country of southwestern Utah. Located near Ivins, this 7,400-acre park boasts stunning red and white Navajo sandstone cliffs, making it a paradise for hikers, bikers, and photographers. Traverse the scenic trails, exploring lava tubes, petrified sand dunes, and captivating slot canyons. Each bend in the trail brings a new spectacle, promising an unforgettable escape into nature's artwork.

Location: 1002 Snow Canyon Dr, Ivins, UT 84738

Closest City or Town: Ivins, Utah

How to Get There: From St. George, head north on Bluff St/UT-18, then turn left onto Snow Canyon Parkway and follow signs to the park.

GPS Coordinates: 37.2178145° N, 113.6395961° W

Best Time to Visit: Spring and fall for ideal hiking conditions

Pass/Permit/Fees: $10 per vehicle for a day pass

Did You Know? Snow Canyon served as a filming location for the 1962 movie The Electric Horseman, starring Robert Redford.

Website: http://stateparks.utah.gov/parks/snow-canyon

JENSEN

Dinosaur National Monument

Step back in time at Dinosaur National Monument, where ancient fossils and rugged canyons collide to create a prehistoric paradise. Situated on the Utah-Colorado border near Jensen, this monument encompasses vast landscapes and over 1,500 dinosaur bones embedded in the rock face. Visitors can hike, raft the Green and Yampa Rivers, and camp under the star-filled sky, all while soaking in the echoes of a distant era when dinosaurs roamed these lands.

Location: 11625 E 1500 S, Jensen, UT 84035

Closest City or Town: Jensen, Utah

How to Get There: From Vernal, head east on US-40 for about 15 miles, then turn north onto UT-149 and follow signs to the monument.

GPS Coordinates: 40.4342761° N, 109.4940541° W

Best Time to Visit: Spring and fall for mild temperatures and ideal conditions

Pass/Permit/Fees: $25 per vehicle for a 7-day pass

Did You Know? The Quarry Exhibit Hall protects a cliff face that contains 1,500 dinosaur bones, some still embedded in the rock.

Website: https://www.nps.gov/dino/index.htm

KANAB

Best Friends Animal Sanctuary

Find your sense of compassion at Best Friends Animal Sanctuary, the nation's largest no-kill sanctuary for companion animals. Located in Angel Canyon near Kanab, Utah, this sanctuary offers a haven for rescued dogs, cats, birds, horses, and more. Visitors can tour the sanctuary, volunteer, or even stay overnight to experience the profound impact of animal rescue and rehabilitation. Each tour and volunteer opportunity brings a chance to contribute to the life-changing mission of no-kill animal welfare.

Location: 5001 Angel Canyon Road, Kanab, UT 84741-5000

Closest City or Town: Kanab, Utah

How to Get There: From Kanab, drive north on US-89 for about 5 miles, then turn right onto Angel Canyon Road and follow it to the sanctuary.

GPS Coordinates: 37.1258243° N, 112.5439256° W

Best Time to Visit: Spring and fall for pleasant weather and outdoor activities

Pass/Permit/Fees: Tours are free; donations and volunteer programs are available

Did You Know? Founded in 1984, Best Friends Animal Sanctuary cares for around 1,600 animals daily.

Website: http://www.bestfriends.org/

Coral Pink Sand Dunes State Park

Dive into the vibrant hues of Coral Pink Sand Dunes State Park, where shifting sands create a dynamic and colorful landscape. Located near Kanab, Utah, this unique park offers a playground for adventure enthusiasts. Whether you prefer hiking, OHV riding, or simply soaking in the stunning scenery, the park's picturesque dunes provide an ever-changing backdrop. The soft coral pink sands and the expansive sky create a surreal setting that invites exploration and wonder.

Location: 95 Sand Dune Road, Kanab, UT 84741

Closest City or Town: Kanab, Utah

How to Get There: From Kanab, head north on US-89, then turn west onto Hancock Road and follow signs to the park entrance.

GPS Coordinates: 37.0474855° N, 112.5263145° W

Best Time to Visit: Late spring to early fall for optimal weather conditions

Pass/Permit/Fees: $10 per vehicle for a day pass

Did You Know? The dunes are estimated to be between 10,000 and 15,000 years old, formed by the erosion of Navajo sandstone.

Website: https://www.visitutah.com/Places-To-Go/Parks-Outdoors/Coral-Pink-Sand-Dunes-State-Park

Little Hollywood Movie Museum

Step into the wild world of the silver screen at the Little Hollywood Movie Museum, where the magic of film-making in the Old West comes to life. Located in Kanab, Utah, this museum showcases an extensive collection of movie sets and memorabilia from classic Westerns filmed in the area. Visitors can walk through the actual sets used in iconic films and television shows, gaining a fascinating behind-the-scenes glimpse of Hollywood history. Whether you're a movie buff or a history enthusiast, the museum offers a delightful journey into the past of American cinema.

Location: 297 W Center St, Kanab, UT 84741-3449

Closest City or Town: Kanab, Utah

How to Get There: From US-89, take Center St in Kanab. The museum is located in the heart of town.

GPS Coordinates: 37.0477244° N, 112.5344270° W

Best Time to Visit: Spring and fall for pleasant weather and fewer crowds

Pass/Permit/Fees: Free admission, donations welcomed

Did You Know? The museum's collection includes sets from The Lone Ranger and Gunsmoke.

Website: http://www.littlehollywoodmuseum.org/

Moqui Cave

Uncover a treasure trove of natural history and ancient artifacts at Moqui Cave, a unique sandstone cave turned museum near Kanab, Utah. This fascinating attraction offers a glimpse into the area's rich cultural past, displaying Native American artifacts, dinosaur tracks, and exotic minerals. Visitors can also marvel at the cave's fluorescent mineral display, which creates a glowing spectacle in the dim light. Moqui Cave provides a captivating blend of history, geology, and wonder for visitors of all ages.

Location: 4581 US-89, Kanab, UT 84741

Closest City or Town: Kanab, Utah

How to Get There: Drive north from Kanab on US-89 for about 6 miles. Moqui Cave is on your left.

GPS Coordinates: 37.1211491° N, 112.5639616° W

Best Time to Visit: Year-round, but spring and fall offer the most comfortable temperatures

Pass/Permit/Fees: Adults $5, children $3

Did You Know? Moqui Cave houses one of the largest collections of fluorescent minerals in the United States.

Website: https://www.moqui-cave.com/

South Coyote Buttes

Find your sense of wonder at South Coyote Buttes, a stunning section of the Paria Canyon-Vermilion Cliffs Wilderness. Known for its vibrant, swirling sandstone formations and otherworldly landscapes, this remote area near Kanab, Utah, is a paradise for photographers and nature enthusiasts. Hike through the labyrinthine rock formations, explore the striking Wave rock, and marvel at the unique colors and textures carved by nature over millennia.

Location: House Rock Valley Rd U.S. Hwy 89, Kanab, UT 84741

Closest City or Town: Kanab, Utah

How to Get There: From Kanab, drive east on US-89 for about 40 miles, then turn south on House Rock Valley Road.

GPS Coordinates: 37.0414498° N, 112.5114737° W

Best Time to Visit: Spring and fall for cooler temperatures and less intense sunlight

Pass/Permit/Fees: A permit is required through a lottery system ($5 per person)

Did You Know? The stunning rock formations of South Coyote Buttes are the result of ancient sand dunes turned to stone.

Website: https://www.blm.gov/programs/recreation/permits-and-passes/lotteries-and-permit-systems/arizona/coyote-buttes-south

Wire Pass Trail (Buckskin Gulch Access)

Embark on a memorable adventure on the Wire Pass Trail, a gateway to the awe-inspiring Buckskin Gulch. Located near Kanab, Utah, this trail leads you through narrow slot canyons and into one of the longest and deepest slot canyons in the world. Enjoy the striking scenery, with towering walls of sandstone and fascinating rock formations that create an amazing backdrop for hiking and photography.

Location: House Rock Valley Rd U.S. Hwy 89, Kanab, UT 84741

Closest City or Town: Kanab, Utah

How to Get There: From Kanab, drive east on US-89 for about 40 miles, then turn south on House Rock Valley Road to the trailhead.

GPS Coordinates: 37.0190960° N, 112.0249493° W

Best Time to Visit: Spring and fall for the most comfortable hiking conditions

Pass/Permit/Fees: $6 per person for a day-use permit

Did You Know? Buckskin Gulch, accessed via Wire Pass, is acclaimed as the longest slot canyon in the southwestern United States.

Website: https://www.blm.gov/visit/wire-pass

LAKE POWELL

Rainbow Bridge National Monument

Discover the majestic beauty of Rainbow Bridge National Monument, a natural wonder spanning 290 feet across Bridge Canyon on the edge of Lake Powell. This awe-inspiring, naturally-formed sandstone arch is considered one of the largest in the world and holds significant cultural importance for the native Navajo people. Accessible by boat from Lake Powell or via a strenuous hiking trail, Rainbow Bridge is a breathtaking destination that offers an unforgettable experience.

Location: 32GP+X8 Navajo Mountain, Utah

Closest City or Town: Page, Arizona

How to Get There: From Page, take a boat tour on Lake Powell to the Rainbow Bridge trailhead or hike from the Navajo Mountain trailhead.

GPS Coordinates: 37.0774597° N, 110.9642224° W

Best Time to Visit: Spring and fall for mild temperatures

Pass/Permit/Fees: No entrance fee, but boat tours or backcountry hiking permits may apply

Did You Know? Rainbow Bridge is considered sacred by the Navajo people and is often the site of traditional ceremonies.

Website: https://www.nps.gov/rabr/index.htm

LAYTON

SeaQuest Utah

Find your sense of wonder at SeaQuest Utah, an interactive aquarium located in Layton. This family-friendly attraction invites visitors to experience the magic of marine life up close. Petting stingrays, feeding sharks, and watching vibrant tropical fish are just a few of the underwater adventures awaiting guests. With hands-on exhibits and a touch of enchantment, it's a journey that educates and fascinates visitors of all ages.

Location: 1201 N Hill Field Rd, Layton Hills Mall, Layton, UT 84041-5137

Closest City or Town: Layton, Utah

How to Get There: From I-15, take exit 332 to Hill Field Road, follow signs to Layton Hills Mall, and SeaQuest within the mall.

GPS Coordinates: 41.0786592° N, 111.9773245° W

Best Time to Visit: Open year-round; weekdays often have fewer crowds.

Pass/Permit/Fees: Admission fees apply; check website for current rates.

Did You Know? SeaQuest Utah offers behind-the-scenes tours where visitors can learn more about the care and training of the animals.

Website: http://utah.visitseaquest.com/

LEHI

Thanksgiving Point

Discover a world of curiosity and exploration at Thanksgiving Point, a diverse complex in Lehi. This unique destination offers a blend of gardens, museums, and interactive exhibits. Wander through the stunning Ashton Gardens, marvel at the Museum of Natural Curiosity, or delve into the prehistoric at the Museum of Ancient Life. Each visit promises new discoveries and delightful experiences for the whole family.

Location: 3003 N Thanksgiving Way, Lehi, UT 84043-3740

Closest City or Town: Lehi, Utah

How to Get There: Accessible from I-15; take exit 284 and follow signs to Thanksgiving Way.

GPS Coordinates: 40.4263030° N, 111.8875307° W

Best Time to Visit: Spring and fall for best garden blooms and mild weather.

Pass/Permit/Fees: Varies by attraction; check website for detailed entry fees.

Did You Know? Thanksgiving Point hosts over one million tulips during its annual Tulip Festival, making it one of the most attended events in the region.

Website: https://www.facebook.com/ThanksgivingPoint/

MEXICAN HAT

Forrest Gump Point

Recreate a classic movie moment at Forrest Gump Point, located along Highway US 163 in Mexican Hat. This famous spot, where Forrest Gump decides to stop running in the film, offers breathtaking views of Monument Valley's iconic red rock formations. Capture the quintessential road photo with endless desert expanses and towering buttes all in one panoramic view.

Location: Highway US 163, Mexican Hat, UT 84531

Closest City or Town: Mexican Hat, Utah

How to Get There: Drive northeast from Kayenta on US-163 N for about 43 miles until you reach the iconic viewpoint.

GPS Coordinates: 37.1032980° N, 109.9881434° W

Best Time to Visit: Early morning or late afternoon for perfect lighting.

Pass/Permit/Fees: None

Did You Know? This spot has become a popular destination for fans of the movie, often resulting in impromptu photo shoots along the highway.

Website: https://www.dantreks.com/forrest-gump-monument-valley

Mexican Hat Rock Formation

Uncover the wonder of the Mexican Hat Rock Formation, a curious geological feature near the town of Mexican Hat. This precariously balanced sandstone rock resembles a sombrero and stands out against the vast desert backdrop. Whether you're a geology enthusiast or simply enjoy unique natural wonders, this formation offers a stunning photo opportunity and a chance to marvel at nature's artistry.

Location: 55F2+FF Mexican Hat, Utah

Closest City or Town: Mexican Hat, Utah

How to Get There: From Mexican Hat, drive north on US-163 for about 2 miles, then turn left onto a gravel road leading to the rock formation.

GPS Coordinates: 37.1736669° N, 109.8487685° W

Best Time to Visit: Spring and fall for mild weather and clear skies.

Pass/Permit/Fees: None

Did You Know? The formation stands at about 60 feet tall and 12 feet wide, creating a unique sight that's hard to miss.

Website: https://fourcornersgeotourism.com/entries/mexican-hat-utah/ebf4c6c9-9114-4de3-88fa-98fe121326cf

Muley Point Overlook

Discover stunning desert vistas at Muley Point Overlook, perched high above the San Juan River in southeastern Utah. This remote spot offers an expansive view of the winding river and the rugged, colorful landscape. Enjoy the peace and tranquility of this high vantage point, perfect for photography, picnicking, or simply soaking in the awe-inspiring views.

Location: 62M4+6P Mexican Hat, Utah

Closest City or Town: Mexican Hat, Utah

How to Get There: Head north from Mexican Hat on US-163, then turn west onto UT-261. Continue for about 3 miles on a dirt road to reach the overlook.

GPS Coordinates: 37.2330667° N, 109.9932071° W

Best Time to Visit: Late spring to early fall for clear views and warm temperatures.

Pass/Permit/Fees: None

Did You Know? On a clear day, you can see Monument Valley, the Goosenecks of the San Juan River, and even the distant cliffs of Navajo Mountain from this point.

Website:
https://www.americansouthwest.net/utah/mexican_hat/muley_point.html

Valley of the Gods

Embark on an awe-inspiring adventure in the Valley of the Gods, a hidden gem nestled near Mexican Hat, Utah. This scenic backcountry loop offers stunning views of towering sandstone formations and rugged terrain, making it a dream destination for photographers and outdoor enthusiasts. Drive or bike through this serene landscape, capturing the essence of the American Southwest. The Valley of the Gods' unique rock formations, created by millennia of erosion, create a mystical atmosphere that invites exploration and wonder.

Location: 739C+5W Mexican Hat, Utah

Closest City or Town: Mexican Hat, Utah

How to Get There: From Mexican Hat, head north on US-163 for about 4 miles. Turn right onto Valley of the Gods Road and follow the loop through the formations.

GPS Coordinates: 37.2751970° N, 109.8682558° W

Best Time to Visit: Spring and fall for mild temperatures and optimal conditions

Pass/Permit/Fees: None

Did You Know? The Valley of the Gods was once a filming location for the classic 1925 silent movie The Vanishing American.

Website: https://www.utah.com/monumentvalley/ValleyOfTheGods.htm/

Moki Dugway

Discover the breathtaking Moki Dugway, a dramatic section of Utah State Route 261 near Mexican Hat. This gravel road winds its way up the face of Cedar Mesa, offering hair-raising switchbacks and some of the most spectacular views in the region. Originally constructed for uranium mining, it now serves as a thrilling drive for adventurers seeking panoramic vistas and a touch of history. Experience a unique journey as you navigate this steep and curvy road, reaching heights that showcase the rugged beauty of southern Utah's landscape.

Location: UT-261 Mexican Hat, UT 84531

Closest City or Town: Mexican Hat, Utah

How to Get There: From Mexican Hat, drive north on US-163, then turn left onto UT-261 and follow for about 3 miles to the start of the Moki Dugway.

GPS Coordinates: 37.2739833° N, 109.9395635° W

Best Time to Visit: Spring and fall for cooler temperatures and clear skies

Pass/Permit/Fees: None

Did You Know? The name Moki refers to the ancient Ancestral Puebloans who once inhabited the region.

Website: https://www.utahscanyoncountry.com/The-Moki-Dugway-Scenic-Backway-Utah-Highway-261/

MOAB

Arches National Park

Find your sense of wonder at Arches National Park, where over 2,000 natural stone arches await just outside Moab, Utah. This mesmerizing park showcases unique geological formations, with breathtaking landmarks such as Delicate Arch and Landscape Arch. Hike the park's diverse trails, take scenic drives, or enjoy stargazing in this enchanting desert environment. The iconic red rock landscape, shaped by millions of years of erosion, provides an inspiring setting for adventure and reflection.

Location: J98J+J3 Moab, Utah

Closest City or Town: Moab, Utah

How to Get There: From Moab, head north on US-191 for about 5 miles, then turn right onto Arches Entrance Road and follow it into the park.

GPS Coordinates: 38.6165625° N, 109.6198125° W

Best Time to Visit: Spring and fall for mild weather and fewer crowds

Pass/Permit/Fees: $30 per vehicle for a 7-day pass

Did You Know? Arches National Park is home to the world's largest concentration of natural sandstone arches.

Website: http://www.nps.gov/arch/index.htm

Canyonlands National Park

Embark on a thrilling exploration of Canyonlands National Park, a vast and diverse landscape near Moab, Utah. Known for its rugged canyons, towering mesas, and unique rock formations, this park offers endless opportunities for hiking, biking, and river rafting. Visit the Island in the Sky district for panoramic views, or venture into the Needles district to discover colorful sandstone spires. With its dramatic scenery and rich history, Canyonlands promises an unforgettable adventure for all who visit.

Location: UT-211, Moab, UT 84532

Closest City or Town: Moab, Utah

How to Get There: From Moab, drive north on US-191, then follow signs for either the Island in the Sky District or the Needles District.

GPS Coordinates: 38.1715682° N, 109.7034005° W

Best Time to Visit: Spring and fall for pleasant weather and fewer crowds

Pass/Permit/Fees: $30 per vehicle for a 7-day pass

Did You Know? Canyonlands National Park is divided into four districts: Island in the Sky, the Needles, the Maze, and the rivers themselves.

Website: http://www.nps.gov/cany/index.htm

Castle Valley

Immerse yourself in the serene beauty of Castle Valley, located near Moab, Utah. This picturesque valley is home to striking red rock formations, sweeping vistas, and the tranquil waters of the Colorado River. A haven for outdoor enthusiasts, visitors can enjoy hiking, rock climbing, and photography in this breathtaking landscape. Castle Valley's dramatic cliffs and spires provide a magnificent backdrop for exploration and relaxation in the heart of Utah's high desert.

Location: 424 Amber Ln, Moab, UT 84532

Closest City or Town: Moab, Utah

How to Get There: From Moab, drive northeast on UT-128 for about 15 miles until you reach Castle Valley Road.

GPS Coordinates: 38.6545081° N, 109.4208837° W

Best Time to Visit: Spring and fall for ideal temperatures and vibrant scenery

Pass/Permit/Fees: None

Did You Know? Castle Valley is named for its towering rock formations that resemble ancient castle towers.

Website: https://www.castlevalleyutah.com/

Colorado Riverway Recreation Area

Find your sense of adventure in Colorado Riverway Recreation Area, an enticing escape nestled along the scenic banks of the Colorado River in Moab, Utah. This area, with its towering red cliffs and tranquil river waters, offers an array of activities perfect for any outdoor enthusiast. Paddle along the serene river, hike the picturesque trails, or simply relax by the water with a picnic. The stunning landscape provides the perfect backdrop for photography, while the diverse wildlife ensures every visit is filled with discovery.

Location: JC3R+QH Moab, Utah

Closest City or Town: Moab, Utah

How to Get There: From Moab, drive northwest on UT-279 to explore the various access points along the river.

GPS Coordinates: 38.6044375° N, 109.5585625° W

Best Time to Visit: Spring and fall for mild temperatures and optimal water conditions.

Pass/Permit/Fees: Varies by activity; some areas may require permits for camping or boating.

Did You Know? The Colorado Riverway Recreation Area is renowned for its ancient petroglyphs carved into the sandstone walls.

Website: https://www.discovermoab.com/

Corona Arch

Discover the natural marvel of Corona Arch, a breathtaking sandstone arch towering over the rugged landscape near Moab. This iconic 140-foot arch is accessible via a scenic 3-mile round-trip hike that promises spectacular views and a sense of serenity. Traverse slickrock, climb small ladders, and witness firsthand the grandeur of this geological wonder. Ideal for families and adventurers alike, the journey to Corona Arch is as rewarding as the destination itself.

Location: 82 East Dogwood, Moab, UT 84532

Closest City or Town: Moab, Utah

How to Get There: From Moab, take US-191 north, turn west onto UT-279, and follow the signs to the trailhead parking.

GPS Coordinates: 38.5799139° N, 109.6200579° W

Best Time to Visit: Spring and fall for pleasant hiking conditions.

Pass/Permit/Fees: Free; no permits required.

Did You Know? Corona Arch is also known as the Little Rainbow Bridge due to its striking resemblance to Rainbow Bridge National Monument.

Website: https://www.blm.gov/visit/corona-arch-trail

Dead Horse Point State Park

Find your sense of wonder at Dead Horse Point State Park, a dramatic overlook that offers one of the most spectacular views in the American Southwest. Perched 2,000 feet above a gooseneck in the Colorado River, this park provides panoramic vistas of the canyonlands below. Visitors can hike, bike, or simply enjoy the breathtaking scenery of this geological marvel. With sunsets that light up the sky, Dead Horse Point is a must-visit for photographers and nature enthusiasts alike.

Location: Sr 313, Moab, UT 84532

Closest City or Town: Moab, Utah

How to Get There: From Moab, drive north on US-191, then west on UT-313 to the park entrance.

GPS Coordinates: 38.5054267° N, 109.7294241° W

Best Time to Visit: Spring and fall for cooler temperatures and clear skies.

Pass/Permit/Fees: $20 per vehicle for a day pass.

Did You Know? The overlook is named after a legend involving wild horses corralled on the point, giving the area its eerie allure.

Website: http://stateparks.utah.gov/parks/dead-horse/

Hell's Revenge

Embark on an adrenaline-pumping adventure at Hell's Revenge, an iconic 4x4 trail near Moab known for its challenging terrain and exhilarating off-road experience. This trail weaves through slickrock formations and offers stunning views of the La Sal Mountains and the Colorado River. Perfect for thrill-seekers and outdoor enthusiasts, this route delivers heart-pounding excitement and unforgettable memories.

Location: HFM7+5J Moab, Utah

Closest City or Town: Moab, Utah

How to Get There: From Moab, head northeast on Sand Flats Road and follow the signs to the Hell's Revenge trailhead.

GPS Coordinates: 38.5845713° N, 109.5327795° W

Best Time to Visit: Spring and fall for cooler temperatures.

Pass/Permit/Fees: $5 per vehicle for day use.

Did You Know? Hell's Revenge features the famous obstacle, "Hell's Gate," a steep and narrow climb that's a favorite among experienced off-roaders.

Website: https://www.grandcountyutah.net/655/Hells-Revenge-44-Trail

La Sal Mountain Loop

Discover a scenic alpine escape on the La Sal Mountain Loop, a picturesque drive that winds through the majestic La Sal Mountains near Moab. This 60-mile loop offers spectacular views of snow-capped peaks, lush forests, and vast canyons. Ideal for a leisurely drive, hiking, or picnicking, the loop provides a refreshing contrast to the surrounding desert landscapes and a cool retreat during the summer months.

Location: La Sal Mountain Loop Rd, Moab, UT 84532

Closest City or Town: Moab, Utah

How to Get There: From Moab, head south on US-191, then take La Sal Mountain Loop Road.

GPS Coordinates: 38.5970870° N, 109.3118022° W

Best Time to Visit: Summer for cooler mountain air and lush scenery.

Pass/Permit/Fees: Free.

Did You Know? The La Sal Mountains are the second-highest mountain range in Utah, with peaks reaching over 12,000 feet.

Website: https://www.fs.usda.gov/recarea/mantilasal/recarea/?recid=73174

Moab Giants

Find your sense of wonder at Moab Giants, where prehistoric creatures come to life in the heart of Moab, Utah. This interactive dinosaur museum and outdoor park allows visitors to walk among life-sized dinosaur replicas and explore fascinating exhibits. Located along Scenic Byway 313, Moab Giants offers an educational adventure perfect for families and dinosaur enthusiasts. From the Dinosaur Trail to the 3D theater, this attraction provides a blend of excitement and learning. Unearth the history of these magnificent creatures as you enjoy panoramic views of the surrounding desert landscape.

Location: SR 313, 112 West, Moab, UT 84532

Closest City or Town: Moab, Utah

How to Get There: From Moab, head north on US-191 for about 9 miles, then turn left onto Scenic Byway 313. Moab Giants is located a short distance down the road.

GPS Coordinates: 38.6708232° N, 109.6867219° W

Best Time to Visit: Spring and fall for mild temperatures

Pass/Permit/Fees: Admission fees apply; check website for details

Did You Know? Moab Giants features a state-of-the-art 5D paleo-aquarium that creates an immersive underwater dinosaur experience.

Website: https://moabgiants.com/

Moab Museum of Film and Western Heritage

Step into the cinematic history at the Moab Museum of Film and Western Heritage, nestled in the picturesque Red Cliffs Lodge along Highway 28. This museum celebrates Moab's rich history as a filming location for countless iconic Westerns and adventure films. Explore fascinating exhibits that showcase costumes, props, and memorabilia from movies shot in the area. Located by the Colorado River, the museum also delves into Moab's cowboy heritage and early settler history. Immerse yourself in the legacy of film and the Old West against the stunning backdrop of red rock cliffs.

Location: Red Cliffs Lodge Mile Post 14 Highway 28, Moab, UT 84532

Closest City or Town: Moab, Utah

How to Get There: From Moab, take US-191 north for about 14 miles. Red Cliffs Lodge will be on your right, and the museum is housed within.

GPS Coordinates: 38.5733155° N, 109.5498395° W

Best Time to Visit: Year-round

Pass/Permit/Fees: Free admission

Did You Know? The museum features an extensive collection of John Wayne memorabilia, honoring his numerous films shot in Moab.

Website: https://www.redcliffslodge.com/the-lodge/moab-museum-of-film-and-western-heritage

Potash Road

Find your sense of adventure on Potash Road, a scenic drive that winds along the Colorado River near Moab, Utah. This road, also known as Utah Scenic Byway 279, offers breathtaking views of red rock formations, towering cliffs, and ancient petroglyphs. Explore the beauty of Dead Horse Point, the Jug Handle Arch, and The Portal as you drive or cycle this picturesque route. Potash Road is perfect for those seeking both tranquility and the excitement of discovering cultural and natural wonders along the way. Don't miss the chance to spot rock climbers scaling the dramatic cliffs.

Location: Potash Rd, Moab, UT 84532

Closest City or Town: Moab, Utah

How to Get There: From Moab, head north on US-191 for about 4 miles, then turn left onto UT-279/Potash Road and continue driving to explore the scenic route.

GPS Coordinates: 38.5312923° N, 109.6566396° W

Best Time to Visit: Spring and fall for mild weather

Pass/Permit/Fees: None

Did You Know? Potash Road offers access to the famous Dinosaur Tracks site, where you can see real dinosaur footprints preserved in the rock.

Website: https://www.dangerousroads.org/north-america/usa/591-shafer-trail-road-usa.html

RedRock Astronomy

Discover the wonders of the night sky with RedRock Astronomy in Moab, Utah. This stargazing tour invites you to explore the universe under some of the darkest skies in the country. Equipped with powerful telescopes and guided by knowledgeable astronomers, you'll observe distant galaxies, planets, star clusters, and nebulae. Located just outside of Moab, the clear, unpolluted skies provide optimal conditions for stargazing. Whether you're an astronomy enthusiast or a curious beginner, RedRock Astronomy offers an enlightening and awe-inspiring experience.

Location: 2476 Spanish Valley Dr, Moab, UT 84532-3427

Closest City or Town: Moab, Utah

How to Get There: From downtown Moab, drive south on US-191, then turn left onto Spanish Valley Drive and continue until you see signs for RedRock Astronomy.

GPS Coordinates: 38.5350976° N, 109.5029155° W

Best Time to Visit: Year-round, but clearer skies in summer

Pass/Permit/Fees: Admission fees apply; check website for detailed rates

Did You Know? Moab boasts one of the darkest skies in the contiguous United States, making it a prime location for stargazing.

Website: https://www.moab-astronomy.com/

Utah Scenic Byway 279 Rock Art Sites

Uncover ancient history along Utah Scenic Byway 279, where stunning rock art sites near Moab offer a window into the past. These petroglyphs, etched by early Native American inhabitants, depict animals, human figures, and abstract designs, some dating back thousands of years. The byway itself winds along the Colorado River, providing scenic views as you stop to explore these fascinating historical sites. This unique blend of natural beauty and cultural heritage makes for an enriching and memorable journey.

Location: G9VX+QX Moab, Utah

Closest City or Town: Moab, Utah

How to Get There: From Moab, take US-191 north for about 4 miles, then turn left onto UT-279 Scenic Byway and follow for rock art site pullouts.

GPS Coordinates: 38.5444828° N, 109.6000516° W

Best Time to Visit: Spring and fall for pleasant temperatures

Pass/Permit/Fees: None

Did You Know? The petroglyph panels along Byway 279 are some of the most accessible and well-preserved examples of prehistoric rock art in the region.

Website: https://www.discovermoab.com/rock-art-sites/

MONUMENT VALLEY

Goulding's Trading Post Museum

Immerse yourself in the rich history and culture of the Navajo people at Goulding's Trading Post Museum, a fascinating attraction in Monument Valley. This unique museum, originally a trading post established in the 1920s, offers a deep dive into Navajo art, crafts, and the filming of classic Westerns. Visitors can explore exhibits of traditional artifacts, photographs, and even a glimpse of John Wayne memorabilia from Monument Valley's starring role in film history.

Location: 1000 Main Street Monument Valley, Monument Valley, UT 84536

Closest City or Town: Monument Valley, Utah

How to Get There: From US-163, turn onto Monument Valley Road leading directly to the museum.

GPS Coordinates: 37.0076529° N, 110.2036295° W

Best Time to Visit: Spring and fall offer mild temperatures and fewer crowds.

Pass/Permit/Fees: Admission fees apply; check the website for current rates.

Did You Know? Goulding's Trading Post served as the backdrop for numerous John Wayne films, thanks to its iconic landscape.

Website: https://gouldings.com/museum/

Monument Valley Navajo Tribal Park

Experience the awe-inspiring beauty of Monument Valley Navajo Tribal Park, a breathtaking expanse of towering sandstone formations and sweeping desert vistas. Located within the Navajo Nation, this iconic park is known worldwide for its dramatic landscapes featured in countless films and photographs. Visitors can explore the valley via guided tours, hiking trails, or scenic drives, each offering unparalleled views of the majestic buttes and mesas.

Location: XVJQ+R7 Oljato-Monument Valley, Utah

Closest City or Town: Oljato-Monument Valley, Utah

How to Get There: From US-163, follow signs for Monument Valley Navajo Tribal Park.

GPS Coordinates: 36.9820968° N, 110.1118615° W

Best Time to Visit: Spring and fall for cooler temperatures and stunning light conditions.

Pass/Permit/Fees: Entrance fee is required; check the website for details.

Did You Know? Monument Valley is considered sacred land by the Navajo and has been inhabited for thousands of years.

Website: https://navajonationparks.org/tribal-parks/monument-valley/

Wildcat Trail

Embark on a memorable hike along the Wildcat Trail, the only self-guided hiking trail in Monument Valley Navajo Tribal Park. This 3.2-mile loop trail takes you around the legendary West Mitten Butte, offering spectacular up-close views of the iconic rock formations. Hike through the serene desert landscape, experience the stillness of the valley, and enjoy a unique perspective of this breathtaking region.

Location: Off UT-163 Monument Valley National Park, Monument Valley, UT 84536

Closest City or Town: Monument Valley, Utah

How to Get There: From the park's visitor center, follow signs to the Wildcat Trail trailhead.

GPS Coordinates: 36.9853376° N, 110.1133332° W

Best Time to Visit: Spring and fall for comfortable hiking conditions.

Pass/Permit/Fees: Included in the park entrance fee.

Did You Know? The Wildcat Trail offers one of the best ways to experience the valley's stunning scenery on foot, providing solitude and a profound connection to nature.

Website: http://www.navajonationparks.org/

OGDEN

George S. Eccles Dinosaur Park

Step back in time at the George S. Eccles Dinosaur Park, an enchanting destination where life-sized dinosaur sculptures bring prehistoric epochs to life. Located in Ogden, this interactive park features over 100 dinosaur replicas, fossil exhibits, and a paleontology lab. Whether you're a budding paleontologist or just curious about ancient life, the park offers a fun and educational experience for all ages.

Location: 1544 Park Blvd, Ogden, UT 84401-0803

Closest City or Town: Ogden, Utah

How to Get There: Take I-15 to exit 346, head east on 12th Street, and follow signs to the park.

GPS Coordinates: 41.2378270° N, 111.9379410° W

Best Time to Visit: Year-round, but spring and fall offer the most pleasant weather.

Pass/Permit/Fees: Admission fees apply; refer to the website for details.

Did You Know? The park's lifelike dinosaur sculptures were created by renowned paleoartists to ensure scientific accuracy.

Website: http://www.dinosaurpark.org/

Hill Aerospace Museum

Discover the marvels of aviation history at Hill Aerospace Museum, located on Hill Air Force Base in Ogden. This impressive museum houses over 70 aircraft, missiles, and aerospace vehicles, showcasing the evolution of flight from the early 20th century to modern times. Visitors can explore exhibits on military aviation, aerospace technology, and the stories of the heroes who pioneered these advancements.

Location: 7961 Wardleigh Rd Hill Air Force Base, Ogden, UT 84056-5842

Closest City or Town: Ogden, Utah

How to Get There: From I-15, take exit 338, head east on 5600 S, and follow signs to the museum.

GPS Coordinates: 41.1624984° N, 112.0187072° W

Best Time to Visit: Open year-round; weekdays often have fewer crowds.

Pass/Permit/Fees: Free admission; donations appreciated.

Did You Know? Hill Aerospace Museum features one of the most extensive collections of World War II aircraft and memorabilia in the Western United States.

Website: https://www.aerospaceutah.org

Union Station

Find your sense of history and culture at Union Station, an architectural gem located in Ogden, Utah. This historic site offers a blend of museums that cover various interests, from railroads to automobiles, and even firearms. Stroll through the galleries and discover the rich heritage of Ogden and its pivotal role in the development of the western United States. Union Station's charming ambiance and collections provide a unique glimpse into the past, making it a fascinating destination for history buffs and curious travelers alike.

Location: 2501 Wall Ave, Ogden, UT 84401-1359

Closest City or Town: Ogden, Utah

How to Get There: From I-15, take the 24th Street exit and head east to Wall Ave. Turn right and continue to the station.

GPS Coordinates: 41.2206470° N, 111.9797140° W

Best Time to Visit: Year-round, spring and fall for pleasant weather

Pass/Permit/Fees: Admission fees vary by museum; please check the website for details

Did You Know? Union Station once served as a bustling hub for the Overland Route, connecting the eastern and western United States.

Website: https://www.booked.net/theunionstation

PANGUITCH

Red Canyon

Discover the vibrant world of Red Canyon, a stunning natural gateway to Bryce Canyon National Park. Located near Panguitch, Utah, this lesser-known gem offers scenic drives, hiking trails, and opportunities for wildlife spotting amidst striking red rock formations. Known for its unique hoodoos and striking color palette, Red Canyon provides a quieter, yet equally breathtaking experience compared to its more famous neighbor. Explore the area on foot, bike, or horseback, and take in the spectacular vistas and serene beauty of this remarkable canyon.

Location: 5375 UT-12, Panguitch, UT 84759

Closest City or Town: Panguitch, Utah

How to Get There: From Panguitch, head southeast on UT-12 for about 9 miles to reach the canyon.

GPS Coordinates: 37.7461316° N, 112.3193872° W

Best Time to Visit: Spring and fall for cooler temperatures and vibrant landscapes

Pass/Permit/Fees: None

Did You Know? Red Canyon is often referred to as Little Bryce due to its similar geological features.

Website:
http://www.utah.com/nationalparks/bryce_canyon/redcanyon.htm

PARK CITY

Alpine Coaster

Experience exhilarating thrills on the Alpine Coaster, a high-speed adventure nestled in the mountains of Park City, Utah. This gravity-driven roller coaster zips through scenic landscapes, offering adrenaline-pumping twists and turns with spectacular alpine views. Perfect for families and thrill-seekers alike, riders control their speed as they navigate through the lush forest, making each ride uniquely exciting. This mountain coaster promises unforgettable fun and an adrenaline rush amid Utah's stunning natural beauty.

Location: 1345 Lowell Ave, Park City, UT 84060-5115

Closest City or Town: Park City, Utah

How to Get There: From downtown Park City, drive southeast on Park Ave and turn onto Empire Ave, then follow signs to the Alpine Coaster.

GPS Coordinates: 40.6514013° N, 111.5078436° W

Best Time to Visit: Summer for optimal weather and full operation

Pass/Permit/Fees: Tickets required; prices vary by age and package. Please visit the website for details.

Did You Know? The Alpine Coaster features over a mile of track, making it one of the longest mountain coasters in the United States.

Website: https://www.parkcitymountain.com/explore-the-resort/activities/summer-activities/alpine-coaster.aspx

Canyons Village at Park City

Find your sense of adventure and luxury at Canyons Village, a premier resort destination within Park City, Utah. This vibrant village is the perfect base for exploring the expansive Park City Mountain and its world-class skiing, snowboarding, and summer activities. Enjoy a ride on the scenic gondola, hit the slopes, or spend your days hiking and mountain biking through breathtaking terrain. Canyons Village also offers a variety of shops, restaurants, and entertainment options, ensuring there's always something exciting to do.

Location: 4000 Canyons Resort Dr, Park City, UT 84098-6546

Closest City or Town: Park City, Utah

How to Get There: From I-80, take exit 145 and head south on UT-224. Turn right onto Canyons Resort Drive and follow signs to the village.

GPS Coordinates: 40.6856068° N, 111.5563345° W

Best Time to Visit: Winter for skiing and snow sports; summer for hiking and biking

Pass/Permit/Fees: Varies by activity; please visit the website for specific pricing

Did You Know? Canyons Village offers over 7,300 acres of skiable terrain, making it one of the largest ski resorts in the United States.

Website: https://www.parkcitymountain.com/

Deer Valley Resort

Indulge in world-class elegance and adventure at Deer Valley Resort, a premier winter destination in Park City, Utah. Renowned for its impeccably groomed slopes and luxurious amenities, Deer Valley offers an exceptional skiing experience. The resort features a variety of terrain, high-end dining, and exemplary service. During the summer, the resort transforms into a paradise for mountain biking, hiking, and outdoor concerts. Deer Valley combines natural beauty with top-tier hospitality, making it a must-visit for outdoor enthusiasts and luxury travelers alike.

Location: 2250 Deer Valley Drive, Park City, UT 84060-5102

Closest City or Town: Park City, Utah

How to Get There: From I-80, take exit 145 to UT-224, follow signs to Park City and then Deer Valley Drive.

GPS Coordinates: 40.6225790° N, 111.4850846° W

Best Time to Visit: Winter for skiing; summer for hiking and biking

Pass/Permit/Fees: Varies by activity; please visit the website for details

Did You Know? Deer Valley Resort hosted alpine skiing events for the 2002 Winter Olympics.

Website: http://www.deervalley.com/

Guardsman Pass Scenic Backway

Find your sense of adventure on the Guardsman Pass Scenic Backway, a picturesque route nestled between Park City and the Salt Lake Valley. This high-mountain road offers breathtaking views of rolling alpine meadows, dense forests, and jagged mountain peaks. Whether you're driving, cycling, or hiking, the scenic beauty is ever-present, with opportunities to spot local wildlife and enjoy the crisp mountain air. As you ascend the winding path, each turn reveals stunning vistas that capture the essence of Utah's natural splendor.

Location: Guardman Pass Rd, Park City, UT 84060

Closest City or Town: Park City, Utah

How to Get There: From Park City, head southeast on UT-224, turn left onto Deer Valley Drive, then take a sharp right onto Guardsman Pass Road.

GPS Coordinates: 40.6088425° N, 111.5298029° W

Best Time to Visit: Late spring to early fall for clear roads and vibrant scenery

Pass/Permit/Fees: None

Did You Know? Guardsman Pass is often closed in winter due to heavy snowfall, making it a seasonal adventure.

Website: https://www.utah.com/parkcity/guardsman_pass.htm/

Park City Main Street Historic District

Step into history at the Park City Main Street Historic District, where the charm of the Old West meets modern vibrancy. Stroll along the cobblestone streets lined with restored buildings housing eclectic shops, fine dining restaurants, and art galleries. This district, once a silver mining town, brims with character and offers a window into the past with its preserved architecture and informative plaques. Annual festivals, historic tours, and a lively nightlife create a dynamic atmosphere that attracts visitors year-round.

Location: Main St, Park City, UT 84060

Closest City or Town: Park City, Utah

How to Get There: From I-80, take exit 145 for UT-224 and follow signs to Main Street.

GPS Coordinates: 40.6446174° N, 111.4962265° W

Best Time to Visit: Year-round, spring and fall for fewer crowds and mild weather

Pass/Permit/Fees: Free to explore

Did You Know? The district includes the famous Egyptian Theatre, hosting events and performances since 1926.

Website: https://historicparkcityutah.com/

Park City Mountain Resort

Find your sense of thrill and relaxation at Park City Mountain Resort, a premier ski and summer destination. This expansive resort offers world-class skiing, snowboarding, and a host of summer activities such as mountain biking, hiking, and scenic chairlift rides. With over 7,300 acres of skiable terrain and numerous dining and shopping options, it ensures an unforgettable experience. The resort's charming alpine village atmosphere provides the perfect setting for outdoor adventures and cozy après-ski moments.

Location: 1345 Lowell Ave, Park City, UT 84060-5115

Closest City or Town: Park City, Utah

How to Get There: From downtown Park City, drive southeast on Park Ave, then turn onto Lowell Ave.

GPS Coordinates: 40.6588596° N, 111.5468477° W

Best Time to Visit: Winter for skiing; summer for hiking and biking

Pass/Permit/Fees: Varies by activity; check the website for specifics

Did You Know? Park City Mountain Resort is one of the largest ski resorts in the United States.

Website: http://www.parkcitymountain.com/

Park City Museum

Embark on a journey through time at the Park City Museum, an engaging destination showcasing the rich history of this iconic mountain town. From its silver mining roots to its transformation into a world-class ski resort, the museum's exhibits bring the past to life. Explore interactive displays, historic artifacts, and tales of pioneering days housed in the beautifully restored City Hall building. The museum offers a fascinating look at Park City's evolution and the resilient spirit of its inhabitants.

Location: 528 Main St, Park City, UT 84060-5153

Closest City or Town: Park City, Utah

How to Get There: Located on Main Street, easily accessible by foot from most downtown locations.

GPS Coordinates: 40.6445501° N, 111.4962020° W

Best Time to Visit: Year-round

Pass/Permit/Fees: Admission fees apply; check the website for details

Did You Know? The museum features a recreated Dungeon and Jail, offering a glimpse into law enforcement during the mining era.

Website: https://parkcityhistory.org/

SALT LAKE CITY

Big Cottonwood Canyon

Find your sense of wonder in Big Cottonwood Canyon, a stunning natural retreat just outside Salt Lake City. This canyon, part of the Uintah-Wasatch-Cache National Forest, offers year-round recreational opportunities. In the winter, it's a haven for snow sports like skiing and snowboarding. Summer transforms it into a paradise for hiking, fishing, and rock climbing, with towering granite peaks and lush forests. The scenic drive through the canyon is perfect for those looking to capture breathtaking landscapes and enjoy the great outdoors.

Location: Big Cottonwood Canyon Rd, Uintah-Wasatch-Cache National Forest, Salt Lake City, UT 84121

Closest City or Town: Salt Lake City, Utah

How to Get There: From Salt Lake City, head east on I-215, take exit 6, and continue on UT-190 east into Big Cottonwood Canyon.

GPS Coordinates: 40.6197836° N, 111.7750740° W

Best Time to Visit: Year-round; summer for hiking and winter for skiing

Pass/Permit/Fees: None

Did You Know? Big Cottonwood Canyon's unique geology includes the Twin Peaks, which rise over 11,000 feet and provide stunning vistas.

Website: https://www.visitsaltlake.com/listing/big-cottonwood-canyon/55175/

Cathedral of the Madeleine

Discover the architectural splendor and spiritual serenity at the Cathedral of the Madeleine, a stunning landmark located in Salt Lake City, Utah. This beautiful cathedral, completed in 1909, is an exquisite example of Gothic and Romanesque Revival architecture with its impressive towers and intricate stained glass windows. Attend a mass, experience the ethereal sounds of the cathedral choir, or simply marvel at the ornate craftsmanship and peaceful atmosphere of this sacred space. The cathedral stands as an enduring symbol of faith and artistry in the heart of the city.

Location: 331 E South Temple, Salt Lake City, UT 84111-1295

Closest City or Town: Salt Lake City, Utah

How to Get There: From downtown Salt Lake City, head east on South Temple Street until you reach the cathedral at the intersection with 331 E.

GPS Coordinates: 40.7696583° N, 111.8817207° W

Best Time to Visit: Year-round, but spring and fall offer pleasant weather for exploring the surrounding area.

Pass/Permit/Fees: Free admission

Did You Know? The Cathedral of the Madeleine is one of only a few cathedrals in the United States that perform the medieval service of Compline.

Website: https://utcotm.org/

Church History Museum

Immerse yourself in the rich heritage of the Latter-day Saints at the Church History Museum in Salt Lake City. This museum offers a fascinating journey through the history and culture of The Church of Jesus Christ of Latter-day Saints, showcasing artifacts, artworks, and interactive exhibits. Located next to the iconic Salt Lake Temple, you can explore pioneer relics, view beautiful religious art, and learn about pivotal events in church history. It's an enlightening experience that brings to life the faith and perseverance of early Mormon pioneers.

Location: 45 N West Temple, Salt Lake City, UT 84150-9006

Closest City or Town: Salt Lake City, Utah

How to Get There: From downtown Salt Lake City, head north on Main Street, turn left onto South Temple, then right onto West Temple.

GPS Coordinates: 40.7708603° N, 111.8944889° W

Best Time to Visit: Year-round, with special exhibits rotating periodically.

Pass/Permit/Fees: Free admission

Did You Know? The museum houses the original artwork for The Book of Mormon film produced in 1913.

Website:
https://history.churchofjesuschrist.org/landing/museum?lang=eng

Clark Planetarium

Launch into the wonders of the cosmos at Clark Planetarium, an interactive museum in Salt Lake City, Utah. With captivating displays, exciting exhibits, and mind-blowing films about outer space, this planetarium provides a stellar experience for visitors of all ages. Discover distant galaxies, learn about the solar system, and engage with hands-on exhibits that make space exploration fun and educational. Located in the heart of Salt Lake City, the Clark Planetarium sparks curiosity and inspires a love for the universe.

Location: 110 S 400 W, Salt Lake City, UT 84101-1145

Closest City or Town: Salt Lake City, Utah

How to Get There: From downtown Salt Lake City, drive west on 100 South until you reach 400 W.

GPS Coordinates: 40.7666699° N, 111.9033733° W

Best Time to Visit: Open year-round, with special events and shows scheduled throughout the year.

Pass/Permit/Fees: Free general admission; fees apply for dome shows and IMAX films.

Did You Know? The planetarium features a state-of-the-art Hansen Dome Theatre, offering immersive 3D journeys into space.

Website: https://www.saltlakecounty.gov/clark-planetarium/

Delta Center

Find your pulse with the excitement of the Delta Center, a premier sports and entertainment venue in downtown Salt Lake City. Home to the NBA's Utah Jazz and a hub for concerts and events, this arena buzzes with energy and anticipation. Attend a thrilling basketball game, experience a live concert, or join a community event in this dynamic, state-of-the-art facility. Situated in the heart of Salt Lake City, the Delta Center provides unforgettable moments and a vibrant atmosphere for all who visit.

Location: 301 S Temple, Salt Lake City, UT 84101

Closest City or Town: Salt Lake City, Utah

How to Get There: From downtown Salt Lake City, head west on South Temple Street until you reach the arena at 301 S.

GPS Coordinates: 40.7682681° N, 111.9010874° W

Best Time to Visit: Year-round, depending on scheduled events and games.

Pass/Permit/Fees: Varies by event; check the website for ticket pricing.

Did You Know? The Delta Center has hosted numerous major events, including the 2002 Winter Olympics.

Website: https://www.saltlakecityarena.com/

Great Salt Lake

Experience the unique beauty and natural wonder of the Great Salt Lake, the largest saltwater lake in the Western Hemisphere, located just outside Salt Lake City, Utah. This iconic body of water, often referred to as America's Dead Sea, offers stunning landscapes, wildlife viewing, and recreational activities such as sailing, kayaking, and bird watching. Visit nearby Antelope Island State Park for picturesque views and hiking trails. The lake's otherworldly beauty and rich mineral content create a captivating experience for nature lovers and adventurers alike.

Location: PQPQ+5C Salt Lake City, Utah

Closest City or Town: Salt Lake City, Utah

How to Get There: From downtown Salt Lake City, drive west on I-80, then follow directions to specific access points such as Antelope Island State Park.

GPS Coordinates: 40.7354375° N, 112.2114375° W

Best Time to Visit: Spring and fall for fewer crowds and mild weather.

Pass/Permit/Fees: $10 per vehicle for state park entry.

Did You Know? The Great Salt Lake is approximately 4 to 5 times saltier than the ocean, making it a unique environment for various wildlife.

Website: https://stateparks.utah.gov/parks/great-salt-lake/

Joseph Smith Memorial Building

Experience a blend of history and elegance at the Joseph Smith Memorial Building, a cornerstone of Salt Lake City. Once the grand Hotel Utah, this historic building now serves as a tribute to the founder of the Latter-day Saint movement. Explore its stunning architecture, dine at its fine restaurants, or enjoy panoramic city views from the rooftop garden. Celebrate special events in its grand halls, and delve into LDS Church history through interactive exhibits. This building seamlessly blends the charm of the past with modern-day amenities, creating an unforgettable visit.

Location: 15 E South Temple, Salt Lake City, UT 84150-9002

Closest City or Town: Salt Lake City, Utah

How to Get There: Located in downtown Salt Lake City, easily accessible by public transport or car from I-15 with nearby parking available.

GPS Coordinates: 40.7699880° N, 111.8902250° W

Best Time to Visit: Year-round, ideal for all seasons.

Pass/Permit/Fees: Free

Did You Know? The Joseph Smith Memorial Building houses an extensive genealogy library where visitors can trace their family history.

Website: https://www.churchofjesuschrist.org/learn/joseph-smith-memorial-building-temple-square?lang=eng

Natural History Museum of Utah

Journey through time at the Natural History Museum of Utah, where the past comes to life through captivating exhibits. Located in Salt Lake City, this museum sits at the foothills of the Wasatch Mountains, showcasing its impressive collections in a strikingly modern building.

Explore fossils from Utah's prehistoric past, interactive displays on the state's geology, and exhibits that celebrate Native American cultures. The museum also offers breathtaking views of the Salt Lake Valley, making your visit both educational and scenic.

Location: 301 S Wakara Way, Salt Lake City, UT 84108-1214

Closest City or Town: Salt Lake City, Utah

How to Get There: From downtown Salt Lake City, drive east on 400 S, turn left onto Wakara Way, and continue to the museum.

GPS Coordinates: 40.7641297° N, 111.8226881° W

Best Time to Visit: Year-round, with seasonal exhibits in spring and fall.

Pass/Permit/Fees: Admission fees apply, with discounted rates for seniors, students, and children.

Did You Know? The museum's building, the Rio Tinto Center, is designed to blend seamlessly with the natural landscape.

Website: https://nhmu.utah.edu/

Salt Lake Utah Temple

Discover a sacred and serene experience at the Salt Lake Utah Temple, a striking symbol of spiritual heritage in Salt Lake City. As the largest LDS temple and center of Temple Square, its Gothic and Romanesque architecture commands attention. Although non-members can't enter the temple itself, visitors can explore the beautifully landscaped grounds and learn about its significance at the visitor centers. The temple, a cornerstone of Mormon history, stands as a testament to faith and devotion.

Location: 50 N W Temple St, Salt Lake City, UT 84150-9709

Closest City or Town: Salt Lake City, Utah

How to Get There: Situated in the heart of downtown Salt Lake City, easily reachable by public transport with multiple parking options nearby.

GPS Coordinates: 40.7705774° N, 111.8919146° W

Best Time to Visit: Year-round, especially during the winter holiday season when the grounds are adorned with lights.

Pass/Permit/Fees: Free

Did You Know? The Salt Lake Temple took 40 years to complete, from 1853 to 1893.

Website: https://www.churchofjesuschrist.org/temples/details/salt-lake-temple?lang=eng

Temple Square

Immerse yourself in the spiritual heart of Salt Lake City at Temple Square. This 35-acre complex is home to the Salt Lake Temple, Tabernacle, and Assembly Hall, blending sacred spaces with lush gardens and serene water features. Delve into the history and beliefs of the LDS Church through guided tours, interactive exhibitions, and musical performances. Whether you stroll through the manicured grounds or attend a renowned Tabernacle Choir concert, Temple Square offers a welcoming escape and deep cultural insight.

Location: 50 N. West Temple Street, Salt Lake City, UT 84150-9709

Closest City or Town: Salt Lake City, Utah

How to Get There: Conveniently located downtown, accessible via public transport or by car with nearby parking.

GPS Coordinates: 40.7704323° N, 111.8925384° W

Best Time to Visit: Year-round, but particularly enchanting during the holiday season.

Pass/Permit/Fees: Free

Did You Know? Temple Square is one of Utah's top tourist attractions, drawing millions of visitors annually.

Website:
https://www.churchofjesuschrist.org/feature/templesquare?lang=eng

The Conference Center Of The Church Of Jesus Christ Of Latter-day Saints

Explore the impressive architectural marvel known as the Conference Center of The Church of Jesus Christ of Latter-day Saints. Located in

Salt Lake City, this modern structure hosts the church's biannual General Conference and other significant events. With its 21,000-seat auditorium, vast rooftop garden, and stunning artwork, the Conference Center stands as a symbol of contemporary faith and community. Take a guided tour to marvel at its massive interior, innovative design, and panoramic views of Temple Square from its rooftop.

Location: 60 N Temple, Salt Lake City, UT 84150-0800

Closest City or Town: Salt Lake City, Utah

How to Get There: Situated downtown, easily accessible by public transit or by car with plenty of nearby parking.

GPS Coordinates: 40.7717719° N, 111.8929180° W

Best Time to Visit: Year-round, check for events and conference schedules.

Pass/Permit/Fees: Free

Did You Know? The Conference Center's rooftop garden covers 4 acres and reflects Utah's diverse landscapes.

Website: https://www.churchofjesuschrist.org/learn/conference-center-temple-square?lang=eng

The Leonardo Museum of Creativity and Innovation

Find your sense of curiosity and inspiration at The Leonardo Museum of Creativity and Innovation, a dynamic destination located in downtown Salt Lake City. Delve into interactive exhibits that span art, science, technology, and innovation, providing a captivating blend of hands-on experiences and thought-provoking displays. Visitors can engage in creative projects, explore cutting-edge technology, and discover the endless possibilities of human ingenuity. Located near Library Square, The Leonardo offers a unique space where imagination meets reality, perfect for families and lifelong learners.

Location: 209 E 500 S, Salt Lake City, UT 84111-3203

Closest City or Town: Salt Lake City, Utah

How to Get There: From downtown Salt Lake City, head east on 400 S, turn right onto E 500 S, and the museum will be on your left.

GPS Coordinates: 40.7589309° N, 111.8845602° W

Best Time to Visit: Year-round, with special events and rotating exhibits providing fresh experiences.

Pass/Permit/Fees: Admission fees apply; check the website for details.

Did You Know? The museum is named after Leonardo da Vinci, embodying the spirit of his multifaceted talents and curiosity.

Website: https://theleonardo.org/

The Tabernacle

Immerse yourself in the rich acoustics and history of The Tabernacle, located at Temple Square in Salt Lake City. This magnificent building, renowned for its architectural and acoustic perfection, is home to The Tabernacle Choir. Attend a choir performance or organ recital, or simply explore the historic structure with its impressive curved ceiling and pioneer craftsmanship. Located in the heart of Temple Square, The Tabernacle is a must-see for music lovers and history enthusiasts alike.

Location: 50 N W Temple Street (at the Temple Square Tabernacle), Salt Lake City, UT 84150-9001

Closest City or Town: Salt Lake City, Utah

How to Get There: From downtown Salt Lake City, head north on Main Street, turn left onto West Temple, and The Tabernacle is located within Temple Square.

GPS Coordinates: 40.7704468° N, 111.8931261° W

Best Time to Visit: Year-round, with performances and tours available most days.

Pass/Permit/Fees: Free admission

Did You Know? The Tabernacle's pipe organ, with over 11,000 pipes, is one of the largest and most elaborate in the world.

Website: https://www.thetabernaclechoir.org/?lang=eng

This is the Place Heritage Park

Explore the historic charm and cultural heritage at This is the Place Heritage Park, located in Salt Lake City. This living history museum offers a fascinating glimpse into Utah's pioneer era, with historic buildings, interactive exhibits, and costumed interpreters bringing history to life. Wander through recreated pioneer settlements, ride a vintage train, and participate in hands-on activities such as blacksmithing and candle making. Positioned at the mouth of Emigration Canyon, this park commemorates the arrival of the Mormon pioneers and offers educational fun for all ages.

Location: 2601 E Sunnyside Ave, Salt Lake City, UT 84108-1453

Closest City or Town: Salt Lake City, Utah

How to Get There: From downtown Salt Lake City, drive east on 400 S, then merge onto Foothill Dr. Continue on Sunnyside Ave to the park entrance.

GPS Coordinates: 40.7526353° N, 111.8158093° W

Best Time to Visit: Spring and fall for pleasant weather and full activities.

Pass/Permit/Fees: Admission fees apply; check the website for more details.

Did You Know? The park's Sesquicentennial Statue commemorates the 150th anniversary of the Mormon pioneers' arrival in the Salt Lake Valley.

Website: http://www.thisistheplace.org/

Tracy Aviary

Find your sense of wonder among the birds at Tracy Aviary, an urban oasis nestled within Liberty Park in Salt Lake City. This expansive aviary features a diverse array of bird species from around the world in naturalistic habitats. Visitors can enjoy bird shows, interactive exhibits, and peaceful garden landscapes. The aviary's mission to connect people with nature makes it a delightful and educational experience for families and bird enthusiasts. Stroll through aviary trails, participate in feeding sessions, and learn about bird conservation efforts.

Location: 589 East 1300 South Liberty Park, Salt Lake City, UT 84105-1111

Closest City or Town: Salt Lake City, Utah

How to Get There: From downtown Salt Lake City, drive south on State St, turn left onto 1300 S, and the entrance to Liberty Park and Tracy Aviary will be on your left.

GPS Coordinates: 40.7438995° N, 111.8751663° W

Best Time to Visit: Year-round, with special events and bird-watching opportunities in spring and fall.

Pass/Permit/Fees: Admission fees apply; visit the website for details.

Did You Know? Tracy Aviary is one of the oldest aviaries in the United States, established in 1938.

Website: http://www.tracyaviary.org/

Utah State Capitol

Discover Utah's history and politics at the majestic Utah State Capitol, situated in Salt Lake City. This neoclassical building, crowned with a stunning dome, serves as the seat of the government for the State of Utah. Explore the beautifully maintained grounds, take a guided tour of the impressive interior, and view exhibits on Utah's history and government. With its panoramic views of the Salt Lake Valley, the Capitol is both a cultural landmark and an architectural marvel.

Location: 350 N State St, Salt Lake City, UT 84114-4799

Closest City or Town: Salt Lake City, Utah

How to Get There: From downtown Salt Lake City, head north on State St and continue up the hill to the Capitol grounds.

GPS Coordinates: 40.7774076° N, 111.8881773° W

Best Time to Visit: Year-round, with spring and fall offering pleasant weather for exploring the grounds.

Pass/Permit/Fees: Free admission

Did You Know? The Capitol's dome is made of Utah granite and rises 285 feet above the ground, providing a stunning view of the city below.

Website: https://utahstatecapitol.utah.gov/state-capitol-history/"

Utah's Hogle Zoo

Find your sense of wonder and excitement at Utah's Hogle Zoo, an enchanting family destination nestled in the serene backdrop of Salt Lake City. Explore over 42 acres filled with diverse wildlife from around the globe, including majestic lions, playful primates, and graceful giraffes. Whether you're meandering through the African Savanna, immersing yourself in the Asian Highlands, or taking a peaceful stroll along the Great Apes exhibit, Hogle Zoo offers a delightful day of adventure and learning for visitors of all ages. Its interactive exhibits and educational programs ensure an unforgettable experience steeped in nature and discovery.

Location: 2600 Sunnyside Ave S, Salt Lake City, UT 84108-1454

Closest City or Town: Salt Lake City, Utah

How to Get There: From downtown Salt Lake City, head east on I-80 and take exit 128 for Foothill Blvd. Follow signs to Sunnyside Ave S.

GPS Coordinates: 40.7503666° N, 111.8141741° W

Best Time to Visit: Spring and fall for mild weather and active animals

Pass/Permit/Fees: Admission fees vary; please check the website for current prices.

Did You Know? Hogle Zoo is home to a two-story rainforest exhibit, offering close encounters with exotic birds and reptiles.

Website: http://www.hoglezoo.org/

St. George

Brigham Young Winter Home Historical Site

Step back in time and explore the Brigham Young Winter Home Historical Site, a beautifully preserved piece of pioneer history in St. George, Utah. Once the winter residence of Brigham Young, the second president of The Church of Jesus Christ of Latter-day Saints, this home offers a fascinating glimpse into his life and leadership. With guided tours, authentic furnishings, and historical artifacts, visitors can experience the warmth and hospitality of pioneer life, reflecting on Young's significant contributions to the development of the region.

Location: 67 W 200 N, St. George, UT 84770-2864

Closest City or Town: St. George, Utah

How to Get There: From I-15, take exit 8 and follow signs to W 200 N in downtown St. George.

GPS Coordinates: 37.1113577° N, 113.5848723° W

Best Time to Visit: Year-round; spring and fall for pleasant temperatures

Pass/Permit/Fees: Free admission, donations welcome

Did You Know? This historical site includes an on-site blacksmith shop, adding an authentic touch to the pioneer experience.

Website: http://history.lds.org/subsection/historic-sites/utah/st-george/brigham-young-winter-home?lang=eng

Kayenta

Find your sense of tranquility and inspiration at Kayenta, a unique arts village located in the breathtaking landscape near St. George, Utah. This creative community offers galleries, studios, and cultural events that celebrate the arts in harmony with nature. Explore the labyrinth of art installations, attend workshops, indulge in local cuisine, and experience the vibrant cultural tapestry that defines Kayenta. The stunning desert backdrop and engaging community spirit make it a haven for artists and art lovers alike.

Location: 800 N Kayenta Pkwy, St. George, UT 84738-6323

Closest City or Town: St. George, Utah

How to Get There: From I-15, take exit 6 and head west on Bluff Street. Follow signs to Kayenta Parkway.

GPS Coordinates: 37.1831595° N, 113.7056416° W

Best Time to Visit: Spring and fall for art festivals and mild weather

Pass/Permit/Fees: Free to explore, but individual galleries and events may have fees

Did You Know? Kayenta hosts an annual Street Painting Festival, where artists transform the village roads into colorful masterpieces.

Website: http://www.kayentautah.com/

Pioneer Park

Discover the rugged beauty and recreational opportunities at Pioneer Park, a hidden gem located in St. George, Utah. This expansive park offers hiking trails, rock climbing, and picnic areas amidst stunning red rock formations. Climb to the top for panoramic views of St. George and the surrounding desert landscape, or explore the slot canyons and arches that add to the park's allure. Whether you're an adventurer seeking a thrilling climb or looking for a serene spot to relax and take in the scenery, Pioneer Park promises a memorable outdoor experience.

Location: 375 Red Hills Parkway, St. George, UT 84770

Closest City or Town: St. George, Utah

How to Get There: From downtown St. George, head north on Bluff Street and turn right onto Red Hills Parkway.

GPS Coordinates: 37.1151027° N, 113.5765701° W

Best Time to Visit: Spring and fall for moderate temperatures and clear skies

Pass/Permit/Fees: Free

Did You Know? Pioneer Park is often referred to as a mini Zion due to its striking red rock formations and natural beauty.

Website: https://tracyaviary.org/

Red Hills Desert Garden

Step into a world of vibrant desert flora at Red Hills Desert Garden, a captivating botanical garden located in St. George, Utah. This five-acre garden showcases a stunning array of native desert plants, xeriscape landscapes, and water-efficient gardening techniques. Stroll through the themed gardens, explore the interactive exhibits, and enjoy the serene ponds and waterfalls that offer a peaceful retreat. Red Hills Desert Garden is not just a feast for the eyes but also an educational experience that highlights the beauty and resilience of desert ecosystems.

Location: 375 E. Red Hills Parkway, St. George, UT 84770

Closest City or Town: St. George, Utah

How to Get There: From downtown St. George, drive north on Bluff Street and turn right onto Red Hills Parkway. The garden is located just past Pioneer Park.

GPS Coordinates: 37.1138459° N, 113.5751310° W

Best Time to Visit: Spring and fall for blooming plants and comfortable temperatures

Pass/Permit/Fees: Free

Did You Know? Red Hills Desert Garden features over 5,000 water-efficient plants and a replica slot canyon showcasing native desert species.

Website: http://redhillsdesertgarden.com/

St. George Dinosaur Discovery Site at Johnson Farm

Find your sense of prehistoric adventure at the St. George Dinosaur Discovery Site at Johnson Farm. Located in St. George, Utah, this remarkable site offers a unique glimpse into the ancient world with its extensive collection of dinosaur tracks and fossils. Visitors can explore well-preserved footprints, fossils, and interactive exhibits, bringing to life the creatures that once roamed Utah. Walk through the indoor and outdoor exhibits, learn about paleontology, and get up close with casts of real dinosaur bones. The experience promises to excite both young and old, offering educational fun set against the stunning desert landscape.

Location: 2180 E Riverside Dr, St. George, UT 84790-2483

Closest City or Town: St. George, Utah

How to Get There: From I-15, take exit 6, head east on Riverside Drive for about 2 miles, and the destination will be on your right.

GPS Coordinates: 37.1011653° N, 113.5349224° W

Best Time to Visit: Spring and fall for mild weather

Pass/Permit/Fees: Admission fees apply; check website for details

Did You Know? The site was discovered in 2000 by a local optometrist and is home to over 2,000 fossilized dinosaur tracks.

Website: https://utahdinosaurs.org/

St. George Temple & Visitors' Center

Discover serenity and spiritual insight at the St. George Temple & Visitors' Center. Located in the heart of St. George, Utah, this beautifully maintained temple is a historical centerpiece and spiritual haven. Walk through its lush gardens, learn about the history of the temple through interactive exhibits, and explore the visitor center, which offers a peaceful retreat and insightful tours. The temple, visible from afar with its white spires, stands as a testament to faith and community, providing a place for reflection and inspiration.

Location: 490 S 300 E, St. George, UT 84770-3699

Closest City or Town: St. George, Utah

How to Get There: From I-15, take exit 8 for St. George Blvd, head south on 300 E, and the temple will be on your left.

GPS Coordinates: 37.0999986° N, 113.5774048° W

Best Time to Visit: Year-round

Pass/Permit/Fees: Free

Did You Know? The St. George Temple was the first temple completed by the LDS Church in Utah, dedicated in 1877.

Website: https://www.churchofjesuschrist.org/temples/details/st.-george-utah-temple?lang=eng

SYRACUSE

Antelope Island State Park

Embark on an unforgettable adventure at Antelope Island State Park, a wildlife haven located in the middle of the Great Salt Lake, Utah. This expansive island offers unique opportunities to hike, bike, and view a diverse range of wildlife, including the famous free-roaming bison herd. Enjoy stunning panoramic views from the island's highest peaks, explore scenic shorelines, or take a dip in the lake's salty water. The park's natural beauty and tranquility make it a perfect destination for nature lovers and outdoor enthusiasts.

Location: 4528 West 1700 South, Syracuse, UT 84075-6861

Closest City or Town: Syracuse, Utah

How to Get There: From I-15, take exit 332, head west on Antelope Drive, and follow the signs to the entrance of the park.

GPS Coordinates: 41.0553119° N, 112.2410504° W

Best Time to Visit: Spring and fall for pleasant temperatures and fewer bugs

Pass/Permit/Fees: $15 per vehicle

Did You Know? Antelope Island is home to around 700 bison, which were introduced in 1893 and have since thrived.

Website: http://stateparks.utah.gov/parks/antelope-island/

TORREY

Highway 12 Scenic Byway

Uncover Utah's hidden treasures on Highway 12 Scenic Byway, an All-American Road running through some of the state's most stunning landscapes. From the red rock canyons of Bryce Canyon to the alpine forests of Boulder Mountain, this 123-mile route offers endless scenic beauty. Drive, cycle, or hike along this diverse byway, stopping at overlooks for spectacular photo opportunities and exploring trails that lead to breathtaking vistas. The journey unfolds a rich tapestry of geological wonders, making it a bucket-list experience for any traveler.

Location: 2020 UT-12, Escalante, UT 84726

Closest City or Town: Escalante, Utah

How to Get There: From Escalante, head east on UT-12 E to experience the scenic byway. The route also connects to several other parks and monuments.

GPS Coordinates: 37.7763619° N, 111.6384250° W

Best Time to Visit: Late spring to early fall for the best weather

Pass/Permit/Fees: None

Did You Know? Highway 12 is one of the top-rated scenic byways in the United States, offering diverse ecosystems and geological formations.

Website: https://www.visitutah.com/articles/the-all-american-road-scenic-byway-12

VERNAL

McConkie Ranch

Dive deep into ancient history at McConkie Ranch, home to some of the most significant petroglyphs in North America. Located near Vernal, Utah, this ranch features hundreds of rock carvings created by the Fremont people over 1,000 years ago. Stroll along the trails to view these fascinating rock art panels, depicting human figures, animals, and abstract designs. The ranch's serene and rugged landscape provides a perfect backdrop for an exploration into the past, making it a significant draw for history buffs and adventurers alike.

Location: 6228 McConkie Rd, Vernal, UT 84078-9752

Closest City or Town: Vernal, Utah

How to Get There: From Vernal, take US-191 north, turn left onto McConkie Rd, and follow signs to the ranch.

GPS Coordinates: 40.5454328° N, 109.6386482° W

Best Time to Visit: Spring and fall for mild weather

Pass/Permit/Fees: $5 per person

Did You Know? The petroglyphs here offer valuable insights into the daily life and spiritual beliefs of the ancient Fremont culture.

Website: https://www.roadtripryan.com/go/t/utah/northern-utah/mcconkie-ranch

Utah Field House of Natural History State Park

Dive into the wonders of Utah's prehistoric past at the Utah Field House of Natural History State Park, located in Vernal. This captivating museum invites visitors to explore the rich geological and fossil heritage of the region. Stroll through life-sized dinosaur replicas, vibrant exhibits, and engaging displays that bring ancient creatures to life. Situated amidst the stunning landscapes of northeastern Utah, this museum offers a journey through time from ancient dinosaur habitats to early human civilizations.

UTAH BUCKET LIST

Location: 235 E Main St, Vernal, UT 84078-2605

Closest City or Town: Vernal, Utah

How to Get There: From US-40, head to Main St in Vernal; the museum is centrally located along the main thoroughfare.

GPS Coordinates: 40.4552778° N, 109.5197222° W

Best Time to Visit: Year-round, especially during spring and fall for mild weather

Pass/Permit/Fees: $6 per adult, $3 per child

Did You Know? The museum houses a real seven-ton Stegosaurus replica, making it a must-see for any dinosaur enthusiast.

Website: https://www.visitutah.com/places-to-go/parks-outdoors/utah-field-house-of-natural-history-park-museum

WENDOVER

Bonneville Salt Flats

Find your sense of awe at the Bonneville Salt Flats, one of the most unique natural wonders in Utah. Located near Wendover, this vast expanse of dazzling white salt crust extends for miles, creating a surreal and otherworldly landscape. Whether driving across the flats or walking on its surface, the experience is both eerie and exhilarating. Home to numerous land speed records, the Bonneville Salt Flats offer a perfect backdrop for both adventure and photography.

Location: P4RX+67 Wendover, Utah

Closest City or Town: Wendover, Utah

How to Get There: Take I-80 west from Salt Lake City towards Wendover; access points are clearly marked along the highway.

GPS Coordinates: 40.7371524° N, 114.0375102° W

Best Time to Visit: Late summer and early fall for dry conditions

Pass/Permit/Fees: Free

Did You Know? The salt flats are remnants of the ancient Lake Bonneville, which dried up about 14,000 years ago.

Website: https://www.utah.com/destinations/natural-areas/bonneville-salt-flats/

ZION NATIONAL PARK

Angel's Landing

Discover one of the most thrilling hikes in America, Angel's Landing, located in Zion National Park in Springdale. This challenging trail rewards hikers with breathtaking panoramic views of the park's stunning canyons and rock formations. As you navigate the narrow ridgeline with chain-assisted sections, you'll feel the adrenaline and exhilaration of reaching the iconic summit. This hike is not for the faint-hearted, but the sense of accomplishment and awe-inspiring vistas make it a must for adventurous spirits.

Location: 725X+MM Springdale, Utah

Closest City or Town: Springdale, Utah

How to Get There: From the Zion National Park Visitor Center, take the shuttle to The Grotto Trailhead and follow signs for Angel's Landing.

GPS Coordinates: 37.2591875° N, 112.9508125° W

Best Time to Visit: Spring and fall for the best weather conditions

Pass/Permit/Fees: $35 per vehicle for a 7-day park pass

Did You Know? The trail was built in 1926 and has become one of the park's most iconic and popular hikes.

Website: http://www.zionnational-park.com/zion-angels-landing-trail.htm

Canyon Overlook Trail

Embrace the stunning vistas from the Canyon Overlook Trail, a relatively short and accessible hike in Zion National Park. Located near Springdale, this trail promises breathtaking views of Pine Creek Canyon and the larger Zion Canyon. Ideal for families and casual hikers, the path winds through diverse landscapes, including rocky outcrops and shaded alcoves, concluding with an overlook that captures the essence of Zion's grandeur.

Location: 6375+7V Springdale, Utah

Closest City or Town: Springdale, Utah

How to Get There: From the east entrance of Zion National Park, follow UT-9 west to the Canyon Overlook Trailhead.

GPS Coordinates: 37.2136399° N, 112.9433252° W

Best Time to Visit: Spring and fall for mild temperatures

Pass/Permit/Fees: Included in the Zion National Park entrance fee ($35 per vehicle for a 7-day pass)

Did You Know? The trail is only 1 mile round trip, making it an accessible adventure with rewarding views.

Website: http://www.zionnational-park.com/zion-canyon-overlook-trail.htm

Emerald Pools

Explore the tranquil beauty of the Emerald Pools, a series of three picturesque pools located in Zion National Park. Situated in Springdale, this trail offers a serene and varied hike through lush vegetation and striking red rock formations. Follow the cascading waterfalls that feed into the Lower, Middle, and Upper Emerald Pools, each offering its own unique charm and sense of peace. It's a perfect destination for hikers of all levels to immerse themselves in the natural splendor of Zion.

Location: 722R+C7 Springdale, Utah

Closest City or Town: Springdale, Utah

How to Get There: From the Zion National Park Visitor Center, take the shuttle to the Zion Lodge stop and start your hike from there.

GPS Coordinates: 37.2511206° N, 112.9592612° W

Best Time to Visit: Spring and fall for moderate temperatures and water flow

Pass/Permit/Fees: Included in the Zion National Park entrance fee ($35 per vehicle for a 7-day pass)

Did You Know? The trail to Emerald Pools is one of the most popular in Zion, offering scenic views and a cool oasis in the desert heat.

Website: http://www.nps.gov/zion/index.htm

Kolob Canyons

Find your sense of awe and adventure at Kolob Canyons, a stunning section of Zion National Park located in New Harmony, Utah. These majestic canyons offer vibrant red cliffs, deep gorges, and lush greenery, providing a serene escape for hikers, photographers, and nature lovers. Explore the numerous trails, from easy walks to challenging hikes, all revealing incredible vistas and diverse wildlife. Don't miss the scenic drive that showcases panoramic views of the canyon's dramatic landscape, making it a must-visit destination.

Location: 3752 E Kolob Canyon Rd, New Harmony, UT 84757

Closest City or Town: New Harmony, Utah

How to Get There: From I-15, take exit 40 and follow Kolob Canyon Road into the park.

GPS Coordinates: 37.4534279° N, 113.2253822° W

Best Time to Visit: Spring and fall for mild weather and colorful foliage

Pass/Permit/Fees: $12 per person, $30 per vehicle for a 7-day pass

Did You Know? Kolob Canyons is home to some of the park's oldest and most unique geological formations.

Website: http://www.zion-national-park.info/kolob-canyons.htm

Observation Point

Climb high and witness breathtaking views at Observation Point, one of Zion National Park's most iconic vantage points. Located in Springdale, Utah, this strenuous 8-mile round-trip hike rewards adventurers with unparalleled vistas of Zion Canyon and its surrounding cliffs. The trail, which ascends over 2,100 feet, offers sweeping panoramas, serene slot canyons, and vibrant cliff faces. Ideal for seasoned hikers, Observation Point offers a unique perspective on the park's grandeur.

Location: 73H5+7V Springdale, Utah

Closest City or Town: Springdale, Utah

How to Get There: From the Zion Canyon Visitor Center, take the shuttle to the Weeping Rock Trailhead and begin the hike from there.

GPS Coordinates: 37.2806923° N, 112.9384224° W

Best Time to Visit: Spring and fall for cooler temperatures and clearer skies

Pass/Permit/Fees: Included in the Zion National Park entrance fee

Did You Know? Observation Point offers vistas more elevated than the famous Angel's Landing.

Website: https://www.nps.gov/zion/planyourvisit/zion-canyon-trail-descriptions.htm

Riverside Walk

Embrace the peaceful beauty of Zion on the Riverside Walk, a gentle trail that meanders alongside the Virgin River in Springdale, Utah. This easy, accessible path is perfect for families and visitors of all ages, leading you through lush foliage and dramatic canyon walls towards the entrance of The Narrows. The 2.2-mile round-trip walk showcases the natural splendor of Zion, with opportunities for spotting wildlife, cooling off in the river, or simply soaking in the scenery.

Location: 73P2+4X Springdale, Utah

Closest City or Town: Springdale, Utah

How to Get There: From the Zion Canyon Visitor Center, take the shuttle to the Temple of Sinawava and begin your walk from there.

GPS Coordinates: 37.2908814° N, 112.9473871° W

Best Time to Visit: Spring and fall for the best weather and bloom conditions

Pass/Permit/Fees: Included in the Zion National Park entrance fee

Did You Know? The Riverside Walk provides a perfect introduction to the awe-inspiring Narrows hike upstream.

Website: http://www.zionnational-park.com/zion-gateway-to-the-narrows.htm

The Narrows

Embark on an epic adventure through The Narrows, one of Zion National Park's most famous and thrilling hikes. Located in Springdale,

Utah, this journey through the narrowest section of Zion Canyon involves hiking directly in the Virgin River, surrounded by towering sandstone walls and breathtaking scenery. Whether you choose a short walk from the Riverside Walk or tackle the more challenging 16-mile top-down route, The Narrows promises an unforgettable outdoor experience.

Location: 73P2+4X Springdale, Utah

Closest City or Town: Springdale, Utah

How to Get There: From the Zion Canyon Visitor Center, take the shuttle to the Temple of Sinawava and begin your hike from there.

GPS Coordinates: 37.2853125° N, 112.9475625° W

Best Time to Visit: Summer and early fall when water levels are lower and temperatures are moderate

Pass/Permit/Fees: Included in the Zion National Park entrance fee; permits required for top-down hikes

Did You Know? The Narrows is often listed among the top 10 best hikes in the United States.

Website: http://www.zionnational-park.com/zion-narrows.htm

Zion Mt. Carmel Highway

Take a scenic drive along the Zion Mt. Carmel Highway and experience the awe-inspiring beauty of Zion National Park. This 12-mile stretch, starting from Springdale, Utah, winds through tunnels and switchbacks, revealing breathtaking views of towering cliffs, colorful rock formations, and lush valleys. Perfect for photographers and road trippers, the highway's scenic pullouts offer unforgettable vistas and ample opportunities for exploration.

Location: 1215 Zion Park Blvd, Springdale, UT 84767

Closest City or Town: Springdale, Utah

How to Get There: From the Zion Canyon Visitor Center, follow signs for the Mt. Carmel Highway, located off of UT-9.

GPS Coordinates: 37.1830502° N, 113.0023159° W

Best Time to Visit: Spring and fall for mild weather and vibrant colors

Pass/Permit/Fees: Included in the Zion National Park entrance fee

Did You Know? The highway's construction in the 1920s included the Zion-Mount Carmel Tunnel, one of the longest of its kind in the United States.

Website: https://www.nps.gov/zion/index.htm

Zion Canyon Scenic Drive

Embark on an unforgettable journey along the Zion Canyon Scenic Drive. This breathtaking route meanders through the heart of Zion National Park, offering unparalleled views of towering red cliffs, lush hanging gardens, and the Virgin River. As you wind through the canyon, seize the opportunity to hike, photograph, or simply marvel at the park's stunning rock formations. The drive offers access points to some of Zion's most iconic trails, making it an ideal way to immerse yourself in the natural beauty of Utah's landscape.

Location: 62PQ+RMW, Apple Valley, UT 84737

Closest City or Town: Springdale, Utah

How to Get There: Enter Zion National Park from Springdale via the South Entrance. Follow signs for Zion Canyon Scenic Drive.

GPS Coordinates: 37.2402387° N, 112.9585267° W

Best Time to Visit: Spring and fall for mild weather and vibrant colors.

Pass/Permit/Fees: $35 per vehicle for a 7-day pass (required to enter Zion National Park).

Did You Know? Zion Canyon was settled in the late 19th century by Mormon pioneers who gave biblical names to many of its features.

Website: https://www.utah.com/destinations/national-parks/zion-national-park/things-to-do/scenic-drives/

Zion Canyon Shuttle

Discover the convenience and ecological benefits of the Zion Canyon Shuttle. This shuttle system operates seasonally to reduce traffic and preserve the pristine environment of Zion National Park. Hop on and off at designated stops to explore famous trails and viewpoints, including Weeping Rock, Angel's Landing, and Emerald

Pools. Enjoy the narrated tour as you relax and soak in the breathtaking scenery without the stress of driving.

Location: 6227+86 Springdale, Utah

Closest City or Town: Springdale, Utah

How to Get There: Access the shuttle from the park's main entrance in Springdale.

GPS Coordinates: 37.2008138° N, 112.9868919° W

Best Time to Visit: Spring through fall when the shuttle is operational.

Pass/Permit/Fees: Included in the Zion National Park entrance fee ($35 per vehicle for a 7-day pass).

Did You Know? The Zion Canyon Shuttle was introduced in 2000 and has significantly reduced air pollution within the park.

Website: https://www.nps.gov/zion/planyourvisit/zion-canyon-shuttle-system.htm

Zion National Park

Find your sense of wonder at Zion National Park, a paradise for outdoor enthusiasts nestled in the southwestern corner of Utah. Known for its towering sandstone cliffs, narrow slot canyons, and diverse plant life, this park promises an exciting adventure with every visit. Whether you're an avid hiker eager to tackle Angels Landing, a photographer capturing the golden hues of the canyon walls, or a family enjoying a leisurely stroll along the Riverside Walk, Zion National Park has something for everyone.

Location: 1 Zion Park Blvd, Zion National Park, UT 84767-9402

Closest City or Town: Springdale, Utah

How to Get There: From Las Vegas, travel north on I-15 to UT-9 east to the park entrance.

GPS Coordinates: 37.2982022° N, 113.0263005° W

Best Time to Visit: Spring and fall for the best weather and fewer crowds.

Pass/Permit/Fees: $35 per vehicle for a 7-day pass.

Did You Know? Zion's name was suggested by the Mormon settler Isaac Behunin, who felt it was a sanctuary akin to the biblical Zion.

Website: http://zionnationalpark.com/

Zion-Mt. Carmel Tunnel

Navigate through the engineering marvel that is the Zion-Mt. Carmel Tunnel. This 1.1-mile tunnel, completed in 1930, cuts through the sandstone cliffs of Zion National Park, offering a thrilling journey with dramatic windows carved into the rock. As you approach the tunnel, prepare for a captivating experience where man-made structures blend seamlessly with natural beauty. The tunnel connects Zion Canyon to the park's east side, leading you to new adventures and stunning vistas.

Location: 626R+GP Hurricane, Utah

Closest City or Town: Springdale, Utah

How to Get There: From the South Entrance, travel east on Zion-Mt. Carmel Highway until you reach the tunnel.

GPS Coordinates: 37.2098139° N, 112.9564538° W

Best Time to Visit: Year-round, but check for weather-related closures in winter.

Pass/Permit/Fees: Included in Zion National Park entrance fee.

Did You Know? The tunnel was once the longest of its kind in the United States, a testament to early 20th-century engineering.

Website: https://www.nps.gov/zion/learn/news/zion-mount-carmel-highway-reopens-after-road-construction-on-saturday-april-27th.htm

Zion's Main Canyon

Immerse yourself in the natural splendor of Zion's Main Canyon, the heart and soul of Zion National Park. As you explore this majestic canyon, you'll find towering cliffs, verdant trails, and the serene Virgin River weaving its way through the landscape. Hike the iconic Narrows, feel the thrill of Angels Landing, or enjoy a peaceful picnic surrounded by the canyon's towering walls. Every turn reveals a new facet of Zion's beauty, offering endless opportunities for adventure and reflection.

Location: Superintendent, Zion National Park, Springdale, Zion National Park, UT 84767

Closest City or Town: Springdale, Utah

How to Get There: Enter through Zion's South Entrance and continue on Zion Canyon Scenic Drive into the main canyon.

GPS Coordinates: 37.2003660° N, 112.9893400° W

Best Time to Visit: Spring and fall for ideal hiking conditions and fewer crowds.

Pass/Permit/Fees: $35 per vehicle for a 7-day pass.

Did You Know? The Narrows is considered one of the premier hikes in the national park system, offering a unique experience walking through a riverbed flanked by towering canyon walls.

Website: http://www.zionnational-park.com/

MAP

We have devised an interactive map that includes all destinations described in the book.

Upon scanning a provided QR code, a link will be sent to your email, allowing you access to this unique digital feature.

This map is both detailed and user-friendly, marking every location described within the pages of the book. It provides accurate addresses and GPS coordinates for each location, coupled with direct links to the websites of these stunning destinations.

Once you receive your email link and access the interactive map, you'll have an immediate and comprehensive overview of each site's location. This invaluable tool simplifies trip planning and navigation, making it a crucial asset for both first-time visitors and seasoned explorers of Washington.

Scan the following QR or type in the provided link to receive it:

https://jo.my/utahbucketlistbonus

You will receive an email with links to access the Interactive Map. If you do not see our email, please look for it in spam or another section of your inbox.

In case you have any problems, you can write us at
TravelBucketList@becrepress.com

Made in the USA
Las Vegas, NV
19 December 2024

14929441R00066